PROSPECT OF SCOTLAND

PROSPECT OF SCOTLAND

Text and photographs by John Hannavy

JOHN BARTHOLOMEW AND SON LTD
EDINBURGH

Half-Title Page

1 Cowane's Hospital, Stirling's guildhall, can trace its history back to the early seventeenth century, while the bowling-green which it overlooks was laid out as early as 1712.

Title Pages

2 For the festival, Edinburgh becomes a coloured mass of lights. Princes Street Gardens become an open-air floodlit meeting place for theatre-goers where visitors can drink coffee and talk, or just walk around beneath the Castle Rock.

Contents Page

3 Lady Stair Close is one of a number of charming little precincts off Edinburgh's Royal Mile. The narrow entry leads to Lady Stairs' House, built in 1622 and now a museum of literature containing some interesting early manuscripts.

Acknowledgements

I should like to thank the following for their assistance in the production of the photographs in this book:

Hopetoun Estates Development Company
The Curator, Mellerstain House
The Directors, Crieff Highland Games
W. D. Pickersgill, Innerpeffray Library
The Tullibardine Distillery
Arthur Dickson & Co., Galashiels
Tormiston Mill, Orkney

I should like the express my thanks also to Dave Lewis, Hugh Roberts, my wife Eileen and my parents for all their help.

John Hannavy

First published in Great Britain 1974
by John Bartholomew & Son Ltd.,
12 Duncan Street, Edinburgh, EH9 1TA
and at 216 High Street, Bromley, BR1 1PW

Contents

1 Inland Waters
page 6

2 Edinburgh
page 22

3 Monuments
page 36

4 The Countryside
page 48

5 The Churches
page 64

6 The Seashore
page 74

7 The Villages & Towns
page 86

8 Maps & Index
page 97

4 Loch Awe, one of the most spectacular lochs in Scotland, changes in character from one end to the other. At the north-east limit of the loch, it is a broad expanse of water dotted with islands while, at the other, the loch narrows down to only a few yards as it cuts its path through high, steep mountains. Kilchurn Castle, a Campbell stronghold in the Middle Ages, was built in 1440.

1 Inland Waters

Think of Scotland and you immediately picture long, deep lochs with steeply rising shorelines bounded by high, rugged mountains. These long fingers of water that penetrate far into the midst of the Highlands are Scotland's special attraction. Someone has probably counted them: they must total hundreds. Some are long, wide and world famous like Loch Lomond; some small and peaceful like Loch Restil—so small that most maps omit it.

The lochs are constantly fed by a thousand rapid, tumbling streams and give birth to a hundred majestic rivers—the Tay, the Earn and countless others. As these rivers flow out of their parent lochs and wind and fall down through the hills to merge and move on towards the sea, they pass through and enhance some of the finest scenery to be found anywhere in the world.

Each stretch of water has its own special character. The Forth, almost meeting itself as it meanders slowly through nearly complete circles, passes under the most famous bridges in Scotland. The Braan, fast and fierce as it roars through narrow gorges, makes a spectacular show as it tumbles down the rocky hillsides near Dunkeld. The Spey, silent and with a slightly brown tint yet clear and sparkling, offers a rich yield of fine salmon to the lucky fisherman in addition to spectacular views for the traveller.

The ever-changing climate of Scotland causes her waters to vary continually in mood. A sudden wind can whip calm waters into an almost tidal frenzy as waves lash the smooth shores. As the sun sets, the lochs become first silver, then golden, and finally black and forbidding, except that is to the fishermen, who each evening set out in their small rowing boats to drift gently through the night. Dawn breaks over small groups of cold anglers, some elated by a successful night's fishing, others with only stories to justify their night's endurance.

Pleasure craft line the shores of some of the lochs during the week, ready for weekend use. Loch Earn and Loch Lomond both share this enthusiasm, including the growing sport of water-skiing. Others such as Loch Lubnaig, Loch Voil and Loch Dochart are noticeable for their absence of boats while their shores are dotted with cars, and with picnickers lying back in the tranquil surroundings to dream awhile.

But we must not ignore the small ponds, the tiny burns, the streams and other small stretches of water that abound in the Scottish hills. They all form part of the overall picture we know as Scotland, and without them the charm of the country would be noticeably impaired.

5 The Caledonian Canal is, in reality, a series of short canals linking the Moray Firth, via Lochs Ness, Lochy and Linnhe, with the Firth of Lorne. It provides a waterway which cuts diagonally across the Scottish Highlands. Used mainly for pleasure craft nowadays, the Canal was originally built for commercial traffic and was one of the engineering achievements of Thomas Telford, the eminent Scottish engineer.

6 *above :* Loch Lubnaig, a small but very beautiful loch near Callander on the edge of the Trossachs, feeds the River Leny from its silvery waters.

7 Airthrey Loch, set amidst the new buildings of the University of Stirling's campus, helps to make this one of the most beautiful University sites in the country.

8 Loch Lochy, north of Spean Bridge and one of the lochs of the chain which form the Caledonian Canal, is a small loch. However, it more than compensates in beauty for its lack of impressive dimensions.

9 The Keir Burn is just one of thousands of little streams which merge to form the great rivers of Scotland. Seen here near the Tayside village of Braco, the Keir flows on to merge with the Allan three miles south. The Allan joins the Forth before these waters reach the sea.

10 and **11** *above and top right:* The River Knaick tumbles
down over several waterfalls before continuing towards
Greenloaning. There it flows parallel to the Allan for a few
hundred yards before finally merging with it. Like so many
features of the Scottish landscape, the weather plays a major
role in its appearance. Lush and warm in spring, the river
becomes cold and forbidding **11** in the dull light of a
winter's afternoon.

12 Loch Ness, famous for its monster, has some very peaceful corners. This view, taken from a point just south of Invermoriston, is typical of the south end of the loch. Further north, the deep waters are flanked by steep mountains and breathtaking scenery.

13 The clear, bright waters of the Spey are home to the finest salmon in British waters. Standing beside the water, or high above it on the bridge, one can see hundreds of these majestic fish weaving their way among the stones and currents of this beautiful river. The bridge was designed in 1815 by Thomas Telford and until very recently carried the main road north to Elgin.

14 The River Tay starts its long journey to the sea from the loch of the same name. Flowing north for a few miles, it passes through Aberfeldy before turning south towards Dunkeld, Perth, Dundee and the sea.

15 and **16** Scotland only has one 'lake', the Lake of Menteith, which shares much of the character of its English counterparts. It is a wide, shallow lake with gently rising shores in sharp contrast to the steep inclines of most lochs. It shares the English tradition of yachting and plays host to some large and beautiful swans. At one end of the lake is Port of Menteith, a quiet and attractive village. Ferries sail out into the one-and-a-half mile stretch of water carrying visitors to Inchmahome, a small island on which stand the ruins of the Augustinian priory of the same name. Built in the thirteenth century, the priory was once a refuge of Mary Queen of Scots.

17 *Far left:* The River Braan is one of the Tay's more spectacular tributaries. It rushes and tumbles through narrow gorges and down long rocky waterfalls before reaching the larger river near Dunkeld. One can hear the Falls of Braan, in the National Trust for Scotland's Hermitage Park, long before they can be seen. Heard from the high vantage point afforded by the narrow bridge overlooking the falls, the noise is deafening.

18 *left:* Loch Restil is not even shown on most maps as it is so small. It is a tiny stretch of water near Rest and Be Thankful. After the long climb through the Argyll hills and up Glen Croe, the motorist reaches a flat plateau overlooking the loch and giving spectacular views of distant Binnein an Fhidhleir towering two thousand feet above the surrounding countryside.

19 *below left:* Loch Lomond, the world's most famous 'Loch', needs no introduction, but perhaps this unusual view of it does. This scene is miles from the busier end of the loch and the bustle of Balloch. The setting is, in fact, only a few miles south of Ardlui, one of the many quiet little corners in the shadow of Ben Vorlich.

20 Loch Iubhair and Loch Dochart are really no more than wide stretches in the path of the River Fillan. The gentle shores of Loch Iubhau rise through wooded slopes and up the steep inclines of Creag Liuragan.

21 Loch Voil, one of the Trossachs lochs, is bounded by grassy shores and pebble beaches. At the southern end is the village of Balquhidder where, in a simple grave in the churchyard, lie the remains of the great Scottish folk-hero, Rob Roy McGregor.

22 The Bracklinn Falls are reached after a short walk up into the hills of Callander – the *Tannochbrae* of *Dr Finlay's Casebook*. Callander is the gateway to the Trossachs, Scotland's Lake District.

23 *left:* The Falls of Leny, also near Callander, are not really waterfalls at all but long roaring rapids as the river races down over a series of rocky shelves and into a deep gorge. The noise is deafening, but even so a solitary piper can usually be seen and heard at weekends, his cap lying on the ground, as he plays to the hundreds of tourists who visit this favourite beauty spot.

24 Loch Earn is fast becoming the centre of Scotland's rapidly growing water-sports industry. At the head of the loch, water-skiing is a favourite sport. Championships are held here each year and the skiers compete with pleasure-craft for space on the waters of the six-mile long loch. Along the south side of the water, beneath Scotland's second Ben Vorlich, a narrow road offers superb scenic views of the loch and the surrounding hills.

25 *right:* The bridges that span Scotland's rivers are very much part of the scenery. Scotland has many spectacular bridges, the result of the labour of many engineers and builders through the centuries. General Wade was one such builder who, for military purposes, endowed Scotland with many roads and bridges which are still in use today. His superb bridge over the Tay at Aberfeldy is a masterpiece of design and engineering. It was designed by William Adam, the father of Scotland's most eminent architect. Most of Wade's bridges were built at a cost of less than £50 ($122), but at Aberfeldy in 1733 the incredible sum of £400 ($976) was spent in spanning the river.

26 The Old Bridge at Stirling can be traced back much
further in Scotland's history. The famous Battle of Stirling
Bridge in the thirteenth century was originally considered to
have been fought on the site of the present structure, but
modern historians estimate the site to have been further
downstream. The present bridge is of early fifteenth century
origin and is one of the oldest and most attractive in Scotland.
The southernmost of its four arches was rebuilt after the '45
Rising and the gates and towers that were a feature of the
medieval bridge were removed two centuries ago. The main
road now by-passes the bridge which today serves only as a
pedestrian crossing of the River Forth.

27 The Glen Trool Forest Park in the south-west corner of
Scotland has, as its focal point, Loch Trool. But in the
woodlands there are many little streams, weaving their way
among the rocks and adding much to the charm of this
peaceful countryside.

28 *top left:* Loch Doine is one of the smallest lochs in the Trossachs. It is separated from Loch Voil by a narrow strip of heavily wooded land. From the lochside road, as it climbs the steep hillsides, spectacular views can be obtained.

29 *top right:* The River Cree on a still autumn day mirrors the surrounding landscape. It flows south through the hills to Creetown and out into the silent waters of Wigtown Bay and the Solway Firth.

30 *left:* Also in Dumfries and Galloway, the river Ken flows slowly out of the loch of the same name, seen here near New Galloway.

31 *above:* After miles of driving across the relatively flat countryside of Dumfries and Galloway, one is quite surprised to see the steep slopes of the hills rolling down to the deep blue waters of Loch Trool. Its setting in the 135,000-acre forest park makes this loch one of Scotland's most beautiful.

32 Ramsay Gardens, a tall and attractive tenement block at the top of the Royal Mile, overlooks the Castle Esplanade and Princes Street Gardens.

2 Edinburgh

Scotland's capital city means many things to many people. To some it is no more than an attractive place in which to live and work. To others it is the destination of an annual pilgrimage for the three weeks of the Edinburgh International Festival. It is also one of the most interesting cities in Britain, offering the visitor countless fascinating places and buildings to visit including three cathedrals and three castles. It is a city of marked contrasts: on one side of Princes Street we have a medieval city, while on the other, a masterpiece of Georgian architecture: the 'New Town'. These two cultures are separated by the area of parkland known as Princes Street Gardens.

Medieval Edinburgh looked very different from today's city. Until the last century there was a vast expanse of water known as the Nor' Loch which was drained to provide land for the approaching railway, the gardens and Waverley Station. But on the Royal Mile, much of the medieval character and charm of the old town can still be felt. The tall tenement buildings can be traced back through centuries. The little closes which lead off the main thoroughfare take the visitor back in time to Edinburgh's medieval heyday and into charming small squares bounded by fascinating little town houses.

The major industry is obviously tourism, and the Royal Mile gives proof of that. Wedged into the bottom floors of the medieval tenements, the 'Lands', are countless souvenir and gift shops. It is ironic that the Lands, built at a time when the citizens of Edinburgh wished to keep their enclosed, inward-looking style of life, should now be the backbone of its open-armed welcome to the world. For centuries the heavily-fortified, small and densely-populated old town used its compactness to keep visitors out. In the sixteenth century its dwellings were built as many as twelve storeys high to avoid leaving the safety and seclusion of the city walls. Those medieval safeguards are now the main magnets which draw visitors in their thousands each year.

The Festival, too, attracts thousands of visitors. The official programme fills every major theatre and hall in the city while the 'Fringe', the delinquent child of the Festival, tempts its audience into every tiny hall and basement club for miles around to savour the delights of shows with strange names and even stranger messages. Every evening the visitors swarm towards the theatre of their choice, or make the long climb to the Castle, venue of the world-famous Edinburgh Military Tattoo. By day they make the traditional pilgrimages to the Castle, Holyrood Abbey and Holyroodhouse, up the Scott Monument, and along Princes Street. Yet only a few miles away at the most, much of the charm of the town goes unnoticed: another of Edinburgh's castles, Craigmillar, stands empty and alone on the outskirts of the city, and Corstorphine Church is locked most of the time to discourage vandals.

Edinburgh is an industrial town as well as a tourist centre. Tweed, tartans and kilts are made here, products which sell Scotland the world over. The technological industries are also represented in force and at Leith, Edinburgh's port, the flour and grain trade forms a basic source of income.

33 *top:* From the height of the Castle walls, the visitor to Edinburgh can see the 'New Town' spread out on the plains below him. Princes Street Gardens in the foreground form an attractive setting for the Art Galleries and also shield the approaches to Waverley Station immediately behind. In the distance can be seen the Scott Monument, Calton Hill and, on the horizon, the industrial areas of Leith on the shores of the Firth of Forth.

34 *above left:* Corstorphine Church is a few miles from the centre of the city. When it was built in the Middle Ages, it was well out in the country. Now it nestles in a residential suburb of the capital.

35 *above right:* A dramatic view of the roofs and spires of the Royal Mile, looking up towards the castle. The tall buildings are a feature of medieval Edinburgh's wish to build close to the castle and make use of the protection afforded by that noble pile.

36 Edinburgh's Craigmillar castle stands a few miles from its more illustrious neighbour. The fourteenth-century fortress standing on a smaller but still impressive rock has had its share of history. Here Mary Queen of Scots is thought to have met Bothwell to plot the death of Lord Darnley. Here too the Earl of Mar, son of James II, was killed in 1479, presumably on the orders of his brother King James III. Craigmillar is important as the first castle in Scotland specifically designed to be protected by guns and was the first to have special gun-positions and ports built into the heavy curtain walls.

37 and **38** Edinburgh Castle is perhaps the most famous of all Scottish buildings. So much of the nation's history revolves around it that it is an essential feature of any account of the country. The oldest part of the castle, St. Margaret's Chapel, can be traced back to the late eleventh or early twelfth century. It was founded in commemoration of Scotland's queen and saint, the devoted wife of King Malcolm II, who died in 1093 after her husband had been killed at the Battle of Alnwick in Northumberland. The chapel is the castle's oldest feature by over two centuries, being the only part to survive the Bruce's destructive attack in 1313.

As it stands today, the castle is not merely a fortress—it is almost a complete fortified town; the original castle is now dwarfed by the military buildings which have been added through the centuries to house officers and troops. This enlargement really started in the sixteenth century with the addition of the Great Hall, built in the reign of James VI of Scotland (later James I of the united crowns), and which now houses the Royal Regalia of Scotland.

The Castle today is perhaps best known as the venue of the Edinburgh Military Tattoo which is a major feature of the annual three-week International Festival.

39 The Royal Mile contains some of the most charming buildings in the city. John Knox's House, about a quarter of a mile from the castle, achieves fame as the reputed home of the leader of the Scottish Reformation in 1560. It is an interesting galleried building and is now preserved as a museum.

40 White Horse Close at the foot of the Mile, near the Abbey, is a restored seventeenth-century group of buildings which reflect much of the charm of Old Edinburgh. Once an inn, White Horse Close was a familiar sight to seventeenth-century travellers as one of the staging points on the coach ride to London.

41 The Royal Mile seen from Princes Street, over the Gardens which now occupy the site of the Nor' Loch.

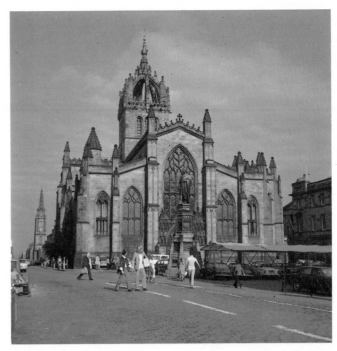

42 The Palace of Holyroodhouse is the Queen's official residence when she is on state visits to Scotland's capital city. By its side stand the sorry ruins of the once powerful Holyrood Abbey, an Augustinian foundation which flourished in the Middle Ages under continued royal patronage. Holyrood Palace was developed by the Stuart kings; James IV decided to convert the then simple guest-house into an imposing palace in the early years of the sixteenth century. It was here in March 1566 that Mary Queen of Scots stood by while her friend and secretary David Rizzio was murdered in her room. It is suggested that Lord Darnley, the Queen's husband, who was shortly to meet his own death in mysterious circumstances, was the ring-leader in this crime. It was less than a year later that Darnley's strangled body was found in the gardens of his house, Kirk o' Field, just after that building had been blown up.

43 *above:* St. Giles', the High Kirk of Scotland, is familiarly known as St. Giles' Cathedral in memory of the few years during which the Episcopal Church held sway in Scotland. Before then it was merely a collegiate church in the pre-Reformation Archdiocese of St. Andrews. Now it is the most famous of Edinburgh's many kirks. Edinburgh has two other cathedrals – both called St. Mary's – the Catholic cathedral in Broughton Street and the imposing Anglican cathedral at the west end of the New Town. Within St. Giles' are relics of Scotland's past glories – fading banners of almost forgotten regiments and their illustrious honours.

44 Edinburgh sits on an extinct volcano – a huge bowl of which the castle rock is but a fragment. Arthur's Seat, a giant slice of volcanic rock, dominates the city. It is claimed by some to have been the legendary home of King Arthur, but any such connections are quite fictitious. The Seat is the focal point of Royal Holyrood Park, a vast area of open country only a few minutes' walk from the city centre.

45 and **46** Leith Docks provide an outlet for Edinburgh's industry. They cover an area which was formerly the site of a medieval village, together with much land reclaimed from the sea. The original village of Leith was built at the confluence of the Water of Leith and the River Forth and has developed into one of the country's major ports. These pictures, taken during an unusually quiet spell in the docks, show how some swans took advantage of the unaccustomed calm.

47 High above the city on Calton Hill stands a group of most unusual buildings. The first of these, a large Parthenon-like structure, was conceived as a war memorial in memory of those Scots who died in the Napoleonic Wars. The designer of this folly, Charles Cockerell, envisaged a massive Greek temple to the glory of the fallen. Although a shortage of money decreed that his dream would never be realised, the existing fragment does enhance the city skyline.

48 *above right:* Greyfriar's Churchyard, near the University, has at its gates one of the most charming of Edinburgh's monuments. The little statue of Greyfriar's Bobby on top of the ornate drinking fountain reminds us of the lifelong devotion of a little dog. Bobby's master, a shepherd, died in 1858 but the little terrier stayed at his master's side even after his death. For fourteen years he stood by John Gray's graveside until, in 1872, he too died. He had been kept alive by the people of Edinburgh who had fed and looked after him. It was they who finally laid him to rest by the side of the master he had loved so well.

49 *right:* By the side of the War Memorial on Calton Hill stands another monument, this time to Lord Nelson, one of two erected in his honour in the city. On the top of this structure is a large ball which is raised each day shortly before one o'clock and dropped exactly on the hour – an aid to mariners who used to set their watches by it. At the same time, a cannon is fired from the castle batteries.

50 The two bridges across the River Forth at Queensferry form what is probably the most spectacular engineering contrast in Scotland. The older bridge, carrying the railway, was built in the eight years between 1882 and 1890. An enormous mass of interlinked scaffolding, it is many times stronger than its duty requires. It could safely support a load many times the weight of the average train. However, when it was first contemplated in the late 1870's, the Tay Bridge disaster of 1879 was still fresh in the minds of the designers and raised doubts about the safety of massive spans across rivers. Nowadays we rightly attribute that disaster to the poor metal used in the bridge castings but the Forth Bridge builders, only three years later, were taking no risks. Their huge cantilevered masterpiece was designed to withstand more than nature could ever offer.

52 Together with Lady Stair Close and Gladstone's Land, Milnes Close (seen here) adds charm to the top of the Royal Mile. These are yet further examples of the enterprising buildings of Edinburgh's medieval citizens.

53 Upper Bow, also near the top of the Royal Mile, marks the site of one of the entrances to the old city. At the foot of the High Street was the other gate, the Netherbow.

51 *left:* The tall, slender piers of the new road bridge a few hundred yards upstream look somehow unsteady against the background of the rail bridge. In the shadow of that rigid and immensely strong-looking structure, it hardly seems possible that these slim pencils of concrete, over five hundred feet high, could ever support the longest suspension bridge in Britain. The wide roadways suspended on steel cables appear almost to float high above the water. Viewed through the steel superstructure, large merchant ships seem like toys as they make their way up the river to Grangemouth.

54 and **55** Sir Walter Scott, born in
Edinburgh in 1771, was commemorated
by Edinburgh in 1844 when this tall
monument was opened in Princes Street.
Sir Walter had many connections with
Scotland's border country also, the
greatest being his affection for his
Borders home at Abbotsford where he
lived from 1811 until his death in 1832.

56 At Causewayhead, near Stirling, stands a tall monument in mock-baronial style to the Scots hero William Wallace. The nineteenth-century tower on the Abbey Craig was built as a reminder of Wallace's Battle of Stirling Bridge in 1297 and contains many relics of Scotland's past, including a sword which, some claim, belonged to Wallace. Historians argue, however, that the style of the sword places it centuries later in Scotland's history.

3 Monuments

If the traditional image of Scotland is made up largely of her inland waters, then it is certainly enhanced by the hundreds of man-made structures which are to be found the length and breadth of the land. The tall, imposing castles which perch precariously on cliffs overlooking the lochs, the small statues which enhance the village squares, and the magnificent houses that form focal points in the countryside all enrich the already abundant beauties of Scotland.

From the prehistoric monuments of a long-lost life-style in Orkney to the ornate follies of the Victorian era, Scotland offers the visitor a strange mixture of buildings. The curious enclosed little village of Skara Brae has small buildings grouped together in which frightened stone-age villagers once huddled in shelter from the unwanted intrusions of both the climate and human invaders; these buildings are a complete contrast to the ornate pineapple-shaped structure near Stirling, erected to commemorate the successful growing of that fruit nearby. The lonely Ossian's Hall near Dunkeld, a hermitage and folly built out of desire for complete isolation, contrasts with the little statue of Greyfriar's Bobby in Edinburgh, erected in memory of a devotion and longing for company that lasted until death.

That man is a complex and individualistic creature is amply revealed in the structures he builds. But our monuments also reflect the foundations of our civilisation, the memory of a violent nation which lived by the sword and shielded its people behind the formidable defences of countless castles. As peace became the rule rather than the exception, the castles became palaces, unfortified and beautiful. The country opened up and building styles progressed. Great architects, Robert Adam and many others, endowed the country with the products of their genius in the form of magnificent buildings for the rich to live in, and for the rest of us to look at.

Monuments, however, are not merely buildings: they are monuments in the true sense of the word, tributes to the men to whom Scotland owes its character. Robert the Bruce, the king who united the country and achieved that great victory over the English at Bannockburn, now stands proudly overlooking the site of his finest hour. Nearby, William Wallace, the fiery swordsman who rallied the Scots in the preceding century, now looks down from his tall monument on the Abbey Craig near Stirling.

Also remembered in metal and stone are the explorers, who added fact to the Scots legends, including Alexander Selkirk, the Fife seaman who became Robinson Crusoe, David Livingstone, the missionary who opened Africa, and many others. Then there are the writers, including Sir Walter Scott, whose novels were all set in actual towns, villages, castles and houses across Scotland, and who overlooks the capital city from his seat beneath the great nineteenth-century monument to his achievements.

The unique gravestone at Innerpeffray, the gaudy crocodile at St. Fillans, the dovecot at Aldearn, the standing stones at Stenness and the magnificent castle and palace in Stirling are all vital parts of Scotland's unique heritage.

57 *top left:* Scotland's other great hero, Robert the Bruce, is commemorated in a lavish rotunda and exhibition area on the site of his most famous victory in 1314, the Battle of Bannockburn. In the precinct is the Borestone, on which Bruce is thought to have set his standard. Focal point of the memorial is a magnificent statue of him on horseback. This was unveiled by the Queen in 1964 on the occasion of the six hundred and fiftieth anniversary of the battle and was the work of C. d'O. Pilkington Jackson.

58 *top right:* From Bannockburn field, the tall rock upon which Stirling Castle stands can be seen a little over two

miles away. Like Edinburgh Castle, Stirling Castle is built on a volcanic rock and is much more than a purely defensive structure. It too contains barracks and other buildings; these reflect its long post-medieval history as the headquarters of the Argyll and Sutherland Highlanders and preceding regiments. The Royal Palace was built by King James V of Scotland and continued to be the Royal Residence until James VI became King of England in 1603.

59 *above left:* The massive gateway into Stirling Castle can be traced back in origin to the reign of James III.

60 *above right:* Linlithgow Palace was once praised as being the most luxurious of the royal palaces of Scotland; Mary of Guise, wife of James V, described it as the most princely home she had ever seen. It is certainly an impressive structure, standing on a slight hill above a small loch in the centre of the royal burgh. As well as comfort within the Palace's eighty-foot high walls, there was also space – four thousand square feet of ground space alone. Scotland's King James I was responsible for its construction and lavished a regal five thousand pounds on it between 1425 and 1435!

61 On the north-west shore of the Orkney mainland lie the remains of the village of Skara Brae, a stone-age settlement which gives a fascinating insight into primitive life in our islands. A fierce storm in 1850 gave modern man this glimpse of the past when exceptionally high winds stripped all the grass and soil off the Skerroo Brae revealing the layout and tiny huts of the village. Since then, archaeologists have uncovered more and more of the settlement and work continues today. The huts, built in close groups to withstand both the climate and attacks from invading tribes, are furnished throughout in stone.

62, 63, 64, 65 Scotland is much the richer for the industry of Robert Adam, that most illustrious of her architect sons. With the assistance of his brother James, Robert outshone every Scottish architect before him – including his eminent father William – in everything he designed. He did not limit his endeavours merely to designing an exterior shell for a house. Robert Adam would personally design every feature of the building down to the smallest fixture and fitting – including the doorknobs! He turned the growing practice of building 'sham' castles almost into an art form. In this context, Inveraray Castle (**65,** *below right*), basically the work of Morris and Mylne, may seem out of place. But for several reasons it played a great part in the future direction Adam would take. William Adam did some of the minor work on Inveraray and it is certain that Robert was present during most of the building work. This first sham castle may therefore have been the blueprint for Robert Adam's future successes.

The other three buildings are all completely Robert Adam. Culzean (**64** *top right*), on the Strathclyde coast, is perhaps his most outstanding. Here he designed everything – building, furniture, drapes, carpets and the many other things that go into a great house. His circular drawing room is furnished in superb fashion, with specially curved tables to fit snugly against the walls.

Hopetoun House (**62** *top left*), perhaps the finest Adam exterior, is located in Lothian. It is a large, ornate house built for the Marquis of Linlithgow and incorporates a less spectacular edifice built by Sir William Bruce.

It was at Mellerstain House (**63** *below left*), that Adam's flair for interior décor came to the fore. Here, in the delicate

colour-schemes we now associate with Wedgwood, he produced a series of chambers of unrivalled elegance and beauty. This was a house that his father had originally designed, but Robert abandoned all but the shell and produced a neo-classical interior decorated with relief plaster-work. The library, illustrated here, is perhaps the finest example of this.

66 Nobody really seems to know when the large stone by the side of the now disused Comrie-to-St. Fillans railway line was first painted. Certainly it was many decades ago. Ever since locals can remember, the smiling face of 'the crocodile' has looked down on them from the hill.

67 The Battle of Auldearn in 1645 was a resounding victory for the forces of King Charles I under the command of James Graham, Marquis of Montrose. The battle was fought over Auldearn Castle and the surrounding lands. High up on the hill, where the castle once stood, is a vantage-point with a fine ground plan of the battle produced by the National Trust for Scotland. Nearby, this dovecot occupies the site of the old Castle Keep. It was built in the closing years of the seventeenth century and housed over five hundred pigeons—enough to feed the laird all through the winter.

68 Borthwick Castle is yet another of the great houses of Scotland which has strong ties with Mary Queen of Scots. After their marriage, Mary and the Earl of Bothwell stayed here for a few days before moving to Dunbar. The castle was built in 1430 and is sited in Lothian.

69 The Ring of Stenness is one of a hundred prehistoric sites which can be found all over the country—especially in the north and Northern Isles. It can be proved that these stones form part of a circle over a hundred feet across but it is not certain that the ring was ever completed.

70 At Innerpeffray, near Crieff, a delightful gravestone is
set into the wall of the churchyard. It depicts the life and
achievements of the mortals whose remains lie beneath it!
Now one of the main attractions of the place, it
commemorates a man and his wife, and their greatest
achievement—four sons and six daughters!

71 *left:* At Dunmore, near Stirling, is one of Scotland's most delightful follies. The huge pineapple-shaped summer-house was built to commemorate a successful attempt at growing that fruit in the mid-eighteenth century. The pineapple was designed as the focal point of a six-acre walled garden laid out by the Fifth Earl of Dunmore. He completed work on both the garden and the summer-house in 1761.

72 *below:* Eilean Donan Castle has one of the most picturesque settings imaginable. Built on a small island overlooking the confluence of Lochs Long, Duich and Alsh, its origins can be traced back to the most violent days of Scottish history. The present building has undergone extensive reconstruction in the last hundred years.

73 *right:* Doune Castle is one of Scotland's most picturesque ruined castles. Overlooking the River Teith, the tall castle commands an imposing position. It was built in the late fourteenth century and restored in 1883. It has seen service as the home of its founder, the powerful Duke of Albany, and later as the home of the Bonnie Earl of Moray. The castle today is used for occasional banquets, festivals and other functions which help to keep the ancient building alive.

74 When Alexander Selkirk returned home to Scotland and Lower Largo in 1709, he can hardly have imagined the fame he would have in the centuries to come. Selkirk, a native of that little Fife village, was a seaman and, five years earlier, he had been set ashore by his shipmates on the uninhabited Juan Fernandez Islands, a tiny Pacific group, and left there. After his rescue, he became famous as the Robinson Crusoe of Daniel Defoe's novel.

76 *top right:* Blackness was the Royal Port for Linlithgow and, as such, was an important town in the Middle Ages. The kings and queens of Scotland sailed into the little harbour en route to their Royal Palace a few miles away and needed protection. This they got in the shape of a huge fortress protruding menacingly into the Firth of Forth. There have been many reasons put forward to explain the 'ship-shaped' curtains walls of the castle. The most likely is that the building was designed with a pointed east face to reduce resistance to the fierce winds which are common on the Firth. It was built in the fifteenth century although much of the fabric, including the batteries and the major portions of the outer walls, are of a much later date.

77 *below right:* The stark simplicity of Hermitage Castle contrasts greatly with the turrets and battlements of Blackness. There has been a castle on this site since the thirteenth century but this present structure is much more recent. The tall keep with its accompanying earthwork defences made this fortress virtually impregnable. It was here that Mary came in 1566 to visit the wounded Earl of Bothwell whom she married the following year.

75 The Third Duke of Atholl appears to have been something of a recluse. He liked solitude and, to this end, built this appealing little folly on the top of a deep gorge overlooking the River Braan. The folly was completed in 1758. Known as Ossian's Hall, the building and the surrounding lands are now in the care of the N.T.S.

78 A winter sunset.

4 The Countryside

Scotland's expanses of heather-covered moorland and her ranges of rugged hills are by no means as deserted as they may at first appear: they harbour a rich wildlife including the golden eagle, the osprey, the pheasant, the grouse, the Shetland pony and, of course, the salmon.

Although such land has but a small human population, it is put to good use in a manner which by no means detracts from its natural charm. It is the home of a rugged, hardy breed of sheep which can live comfortably on steep mountain slopes where few other creatures could survive. They are timid animals, shy of humans, and for most of the year are left to roam whither they will. Their thick coats provide wool for Scotland's famous tweeds.

Here are to be found also a unique breed – Highland cattle: these are handsome, long-haired beasts whose young resemble plump teddy-bears.

The fertile arable farmland of the Lowlands turns a rich gold each summer as it yields its vital crop of barley. Hundreds of acres of it are harvested to be malted, fermented and distilled into the principal export – malt whisky.

The Scottish scene, cultivated or not, is enhanced by its wild flowers. The poppies which spring up in the fields and along the roadsides add a bright splash of crimson to the green of the grasses, and wild cotton abounds in the marshlands.

The mills, farms and other signs of human habitation add detail to the picture. Man's ingenuity often contributes to, rather than detracts from, the overall appearance of the countryside.

The weather is a major factor in the changing scene. As the clouds build up and darken before a storm, they sometimes drain all colour from the landscape and sometimes invest it with an eerie luminosity. As the seasons change, the countryside changes dramatically: the greens of summer turn to purple and gold as the heather blooms and the leaves begin to die. The perpetual cycle of nature never quite repeats itself exactly; therein lies its beauty.

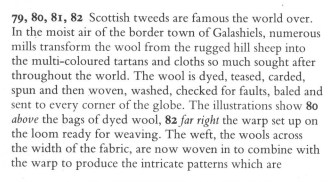

79, 80, 81, 82 Scottish tweeds are famous the world over. In the moist air of the border town of Galashiels, numerous mills transform the wool from the rugged hill sheep into the multi-coloured tartans and cloths so much sought after throughout the world. The wool is dyed, teased, carded, spun and then woven, washed, checked for faults, baled and sent to every corner of the globe. The illustrations show **80** *above* the bags of dyed wool, **82** *far right* the warp set up on the loom ready for weaving. The weft, the wools across the width of the fabric, are now woven in to combine with the warp to produce the intricate patterns which are characteristic of Scottish tweeds. **81** *above* The tweed after washing, ready to be dried and checked by the skilled eyes of the mill-workers.

83 The first fall of snow in early winter gives the countryside a fresh, clean appearance, draining from it the last of autumn's fading colours.

84 The long-haired, long-horned Highland cattle that are associated with the mountains of Northern Scotland are a rugged breed. They are nervous of human beings and certainly do not like people approaching their calves too closely.

85 *top right:* Loch Leven, in Highland, is one of two Scottish Lochs to bear the same name. The other, in Tayside (an inland loch) is smaller and less spectacular than this long thin saltwater loch. The visitor to this part of Scotland, travelling north, has the choice of driving round the steep shores of the loch or spending five minutes on the small ferry which plies between North and South Ballachulish.

86 *below right:* Glendevon forms one of the hilly entrances to Fife. The glen, sometimes wide and pastoral, sometimes narrow with steep hillsides on either side leading up to rocky crags, forms a spectacular doorway to the rich county and ancient kingdom.

87 and **88** *above and centre top:* The Sma' Glen stretching
northwards from Crieff and twisting through a maze of hills
and valleys is another of Scotland's narrow glens. Streams at
the foot of the valley wind round the occasional small
farmhouse: it is not only sheep that inhabit this bleak
landscape.

89 As so much of Scotland's countryside is covered by the fairways and tees of golf-courses it would be unfair to produce a book on the country without reference to the traditional national sport. Gleneagles Hotel Golf Course, perhaps one of the most beautiful in the land, stretches out into the countryside from the enormous Gleneagles Hotel near Auchterarder in Tayside. This course has been attempted–although not always mastered–by presidents of the United States, as well as by local players. It is a favourite of the world's celebrities in the spheres of both politics and entertainment.

90 *Sligachan, Skye*
The 'Misty Isle' has many faces and it would be hard to think of any which is unattractive. Even in the misty early morning, Loch Sligachan, between Broadford and Portree is a scene of great beauty. The soft colours of the almost empty landscape reflected in the still waters of the loch are, perhaps, preferable to the brighter, warmer tones of a hot summer's day.

91 *left:* Just outside Peebles, the river Tweed flows through some truly beautiful countryside, flanked by lush green farmlands. Here it winds round and past the ruins of the fifteenth-century Neidpath Castle.

92 Tormiston Mill stands alone on a small plain on the mainland of Orkney. The surrounding countryside is predominantly flat except for the conical protrusion of Maes Howe, a prehistoric burial mound which is one of the most important archaeological features of the island. The mill is still in working order and today houses a gift shop and restaurant. Against the dark sky of an approaching thunderstorm, the mill stands out clearly by the side of the corn fields that once kept it busy.

93 Wild cotton is a feature of the marshy areas of Scotland, especially in the northern counties and islands. The plant grows unattended, ripens in late July or early August, dies unnoticed and repeats the cycle next season. The moorlands are a mass of small areas of white each summer as the cotton grows to maturity.

94 *top left*, **95** *top right*, **96** *below left*, **97**, *below right*, **98** *facing page*.

The need to grind corn grown in the fields of Scotland led to the development of some highly original mechanisms for driving mill-wheels. At Dounby, the Click Mill was developed: the force of the water running past the propeller was sufficient to turn it and drive the millstones directly, **94** and **95**. Preston Mill, **96** and **98**, near East Linton, used a redirected stream and the 'undershot' system to drive a conventional paddle wheel. This in turn drove the stone by a system of gears. At Tormiston **97** we can see the wooden mechanism which fed the corn into the stones for milling.

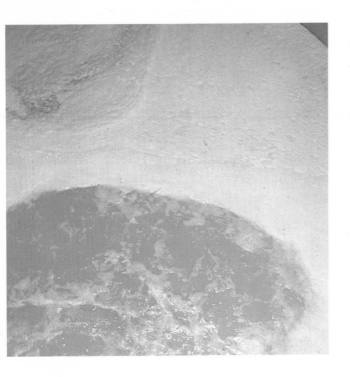

FACING PAGE

99 *top left:* Scotland abounds in clear streams which are the basis, along with barley, of Scotland's major export. Malt whisky—the pure distillate and not the usual blend—is an individual drink. The grain distillate on its own is rather unpalatable but the single malt is the other extreme and has a highly satisfying taste. Malt whisky is produced from malted barley, as opposed to maize for the less notable alternatives. All grain whiskies require the addition of selected malts to make them drinkable.

100 *top right:* The water used in the distillation of malt whisky is chosen for its particular characteristics; the taste is of vital importance.

101 *below:* The distillery will be sited near to that special stream, and close by will be the maltings where the barley is warmed in moist air until germination turns all the starches into sugar. Then it is gently dried over a peat fire to kill the growth and dry the grains. During the malting process, the barley is frequently tossed on the maltings floor.

THIS PAGE

102 *top left:* The malted barley is now ground, mixed with water from the stream and poured into the 'mash tun' to be thoroughly mixed. The liquid is occasionally drawn off and now, **102**, known as the 'wort', it is fed into the 'wash backs' in the 'tun rooms' where the yeasts are added. The wort then becomes known as the 'wash' and it is here that fermentation takes place. The first distillation of the wash produces 'low wines', a raw basic distillate which is further distilled to produce pure and highly concentrated malt whisky at over twice the required proof. Water is added to reduce the proof to about 111° and the distillate is then casked.

103 *top right:* For ten, fifteen or even twenty years, the whisky lies in casks in bonded warehouses, slowly evaporating into the sweet-smelling Scottish air, while it matures.

104 *right:* Further diluted to a proof of 80° or 100°, the whisky is bottled ready for sale. The beautiful colour of a pure whisky comes from the sherry-impregnated casks in which it has been stored.

105 A young deer seen against the traditional background of a Scottish loch.

106 Lochen na h'Achlaise is the name given to an area of bog-land and water alongside the main road over the moors south of Glencoe. Many tourists use this route on their way to the mountains and the ski resorts and, perhaps, in their haste, pass by this beautiful spot without stopping to admire the views.

107 *right*: A Galloway farmhouse nestling at the foot of a heavily-wooded hillside is served by an attractive little bridge over a clear right burn.

5 The Churches

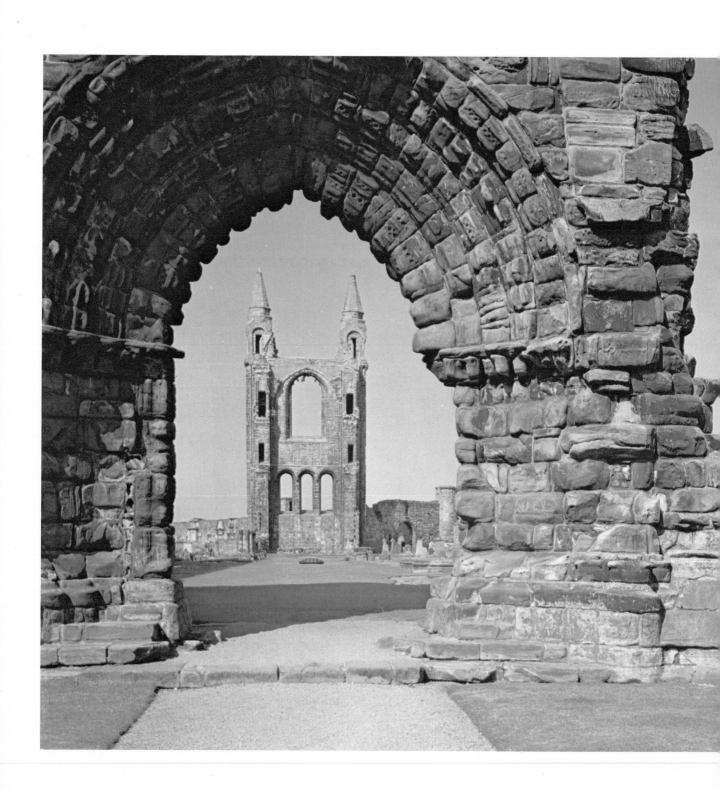

Scotland owes so much of her heritage to the monks and clerics who lived on her lands in the past centuries that it would be almost unthinkable to ignore them in any book on the country. It was they who first brought organised farming to Scotland and with it the first economic agricultural communities. Their majestic abbeys and priories, their cathedrals and churches became the focal points of the regions in which they were sited. In many cases, civil communities sprang up outside their walls. They were the landowners and the scholars.

From end to end, the country offers the visitor hundreds of medieval churches to visit; some are simple, some ornate and imposing. Many are in ruins while others are still in use and as worthy of our attention as the greatest churches in more prosperous and flamboyant England.

The Scottish climate and the Scottish people are liable to greater extremes than their English counterparts and for that reason the country's ecclesiastical heritage is less complete than that south of the border. Many churches were destroyed after the Reformation, or stripped of their lead roofs and left to the ravages of the weather. St. Andrews Cathedral, roofless and at the mercy of the elements, lasted only until the first violent storm when ferocious winds blew down its mighty walls. Other churches were more lucky. They were modified and made to serve the new rites; in their cases, at worst, only the choir was left to decay. Yet others were too remote to warrant visits from the lead and stone thieves. And finally there were those which, though they ceased to function as churches, continued their lives as stores, boat-houses, police stations, halls or prisons or for whatever other purpose best served the communities at the time. St. Giles' Cathedral in Edinburgh served as a police station and prison before being restored to ecclesiastical use. In Kirkwall, in the Orkney Islands, the cathedral served as a boat-house. Stirling's Holy Rude was divided into two smaller churches only to be reunited centuries later.

The architecture of these massive piles reflects the ever-changing and developing styles of the Middle Ages. The accepted European styles were given a unique Scottish interpretation. The design is more severe, the decoration more restrained and the scale usually much reduced. Only in a few cases is the flamboyance of the English and French ever mirrored. In Dunblane, where the west door shows obvious French influence, the extravagance is lacking although the style is there. Dunfermline echoes the singularity of Durham with an architectural licence which is only equalled in one other church, for the Dunfermline masons had also built Durham – and perhaps Lindisfarne too.

There is only one example in Scotland of a large and decorated building – at Elgin, where the stark ruins of the great cathedral are reminder enough of the one-time splendour of this most important church.

108 The ruins which stand overlooking the harbour and the sea in the Fife city of St. Andrews are all that remain of the longest and most important church ever built in Scotland. The great cathedral and priory of the Augustinian Canons which was founded in the twelfth century was built near the original St. Rule's Church, the tower of which still stands near by. From the top of St. Rule's Tower, superb views of the city can be seen, together with a complete ground plan of the great cathedral below. The nearby Royal and Ancient Golf Club is the traditional home of the game and the club itself was founded in 1754.

109 The ruins of Elgin Cathedral hardly do justice to the once magnificent church. The church dates back to the thirteenth century and there is proof that a church stood on this site for two centuries before that. Elgin Cathedral was one of the unfortunates which suffered in the years immediately following the Reformation – the lead was stripped from the roof and processes of decay started very shortly afterwards.

110 According to the Orkneyinga Saga, Magnus, the patron saint of this ancient cathedral, was a young Norwegian nobleman. King Magnus of the Norwegians brought the young Magnus Erlendson with him to Britain on his voyage in 1098. Before a battle on Anglesey, young Magnus refused to take up arms and fight and, instead, took up his prayer book. After the king's death, he returned to Orkney. A disagreement between the now Earl Magnus and his cousin Earl Hakon led to a bitter feud in which Hakon was convinced by his associates that the only way to ensure his personal safety was to be rid of Magnus. Magnus, a gentle man who bore no malice to any person, was eventually murdered with a single axe blow to the head and was subsequently mourned as a martyr by the local population. His murder is traditionally believed to have taken place on 16th April, 1117. The Cathedral Church of St. Magnus in Kirkwall was founded by Earl Rognvald, Magnus's nephew, and work started on the building twenty years after the murder. Today we have a splendid Romanesque monument built in the attractive local red, yellow and grey stones. The church has been used for various purposes – meeting place and boat-store to list but two – during its long history.

111 Dalmeny Church is situated only a few miles from Edinburgh, a fact which was to help greatly in presenting today's generation with the fine building in its present state. The original Romanesque church stood for centuries without a tower and by the beginning of this century the only traces of the tower were below ground level. It is not even certain if the tower ever existed in medieval days. An ambitious minister was appointed to the charge half a century ago and set about the task of building a tower; there his problems started. He found the original designs and the name of the quarry whence the church stone had come in the twelfth century, but the quarry was no longer productive. By a happy coincidence, Calton Prison in Edinburgh, built of the same stone, was being demolished at the time, so the prison stones were moved out to Dalmeny and the tower built to blend perfectly with a church built over seven hundred years earlier.

112 *top left:* Another church which has been used for various purposes is Stirling's Church of the Holy Rude. This beautiful part-Romanesque, part-Gothic structure situated on Stirling's rock just beneath the castle is perhaps best known as the only surviving coronation church in Scotland.

113 *top right:* Glasgow Cathedral. The present building externally at least, is predominantly of nineteenth century origin, being the result of extensive renovation and alteration at the hands of rather ill-advised 'restorers'. However, inside, this large church retains much of its medieval character and splendour.

114 Near the Royal Palace and fortress of Linlithgow stands the parish church of St. Michael. This splendidly proportioned Gothic Church originally sported a stone corona which was removed when it became unsafe. For years there was no crown on the top of the tower until the present gold structure was built in 1964, one hundred and forty-three years after the removal of the original. It was designed by Geoffrey Clarke A.R.C.A. and is made of laminated wood clad in aluminium. The church itself was dedicated in 1242 – almost two hundred years before the palace was built. It was the medieval practice to restore or replace the fabric of buildings in the style current at the time of the restoration.

115 Six miles from Linlithgow is the medieval home of the Knights Hospitaller of the Order of St. John of Jerusalem. Only the transepts of the once rich and powerful Torphichen Preceptory remain today. An interesting feature of the site is the 'refuge stone' which marked one of the limits of the sanctuary afforded by the church. There was a medieval custom of extending sanctuary to anyone within the confines of an area bounded by four such stones and there criminals and other fugitives from justice were safe from pursuit and capture.

Dunblane Cathedral, one of Scotland's finest medieval relics, stood roofless and deserted for centuries. The church, markedly French in style, is small by English standards but, despite its lack of stature, it is beautifully proportioned. The see was founded here in the twelfth century but the fabric, with a few exceptions such as part of the tower, dates from the thirteenth and fifteenth centuries. The choir interior dates from the late thirteenth or early fourteenth century although the screen, **118** *right,* is modern. The tower, **116** *above,* in its original form was built around 1100 and the base of the present structure can be traced back to that period. As we progress up the tower, we move forward century by century to culminate in the sixteenth-century parapet, built by Bishop Chisholm. The West Door, **117** *right,* pure, pointed Gothic architecture, is one of the architectural treasures of Scotland's medieval Church.

One of the most famous groups of buildings in Scotland is not, geographically speaking, a group at all. The Border Abbeys—Kelso, Melrose, Dryburgh and Jedburgh—all sited within a few miles of each other, can be found in Borders. Kelso, once the most powerful of the four, is now the most ruined: only a tall fragment of the choir and transepts still stands, hemmed in by more modern buildings. The three illustrations here, however, show the abbeys which have survived a little better. Dryburgh, **119** *top left,* an abbey founded by the Premonstratensian Canons, now houses the graves of Sir Walter Scott and Field Marshall Earl Haig in the ruined transepts of her twelfth-century church. At Melrose, **120** *below left,* only the church has survived to any great extent— and here most of the nave has been lost. Melrose's twelfth-century church was used as the parish church for the town until 1810 and it is for this reason that so much of it, although somewhat disfigured by clumsy additions, has survived. The Augustinian abbey at Jedburgh, **121** *right,* was built overlooking Jed Water, a tributary of the Teviot, and the tall abbey church stands isolated today amidst the foundations of Conventual buildings. The Augustinians first moved here in 1138 and, like all the other border abbeys, had a violent existence, suffering frequent English raids before they finally abandoned the site in the mid-sixteenth century.

122 Fishing boats at anchor in one of Fife's many harbours.
The picturesque little boats, whose home port is Kirkcaldy,
fish in the North Sea in almost all weathers.

6 The Seashore

The sea has always played a vital role in the development of the Scottish nation. From the earliest colonisation of Scotland, through the invasions of the past centuries, right up to the present time, the fact of being a nation almost entirely bounded by water has been in the forefront of Scottish minds. It was by sea that the Vikings invaded first Orkney then the mainland. It was off the Scottish coast that many ships, Scottish, English, French and Spanish, met their doom in the Middle Ages. And during both World Wars the coast has played a vital role in both defence and offence. The naval bases of Rosyth and Scapa Flow were, until the end of the last war, the major centres of British naval power. Now, in peacetime, only the scars and debris of war remain at Scapa while Rosyth still plays host to a much depleted navy on the Firth of Forth.

The character of the seashore is varied, sometimes rugged and dangerous to ships and sailors, sometimes gentle. The rolling dunes of Lothian contrast vividly with the dangerous rocks of Borders only a few miles south. The Fife coast too offers similar striking variations.

Around the perimeter of the island of Hoy, up in the Northern Isles, are the tallest cliffs in Scotland, towering fifteen hundred feet above the raging seas of the Pentland Firth. The Firth can be calm one moment and be whipped up into a storm of huge rolling waves the next, tossing the tiny Orkney ferry in their wake. The traveller can leave the shelter of Scrabster in calm seas and bright sunlight and find himself in swelling seas and dense fog only a mile offshore—to return to light and calm as the vessel rounds Hoy and prepares to tie up at Stromness pier. Every inlet in the jagged twisting coastline holds a well-constructed haven for fishing boats. Usually the entrances are small, with room enough only to admit the tiny craft escaping from the threatening temper of the sea. The fishermen in these waters are a hardy breed, prepared for sudden changes in the mood of the sea. Their little wooden craft are built to weather the sometimes frightening storms though they may have to seek refuge in any of the hundreds of tiny sheltered harbours, whose narrow entrances fit them for use only by small craft. After a night accepting all the seas can offer them, these brave men return to port with their catches of herring, cod, haddock and sole, or perhaps lobster and crab, to offer them for sale in the quayside fish markets.

Giant merchant craft, more capable of standing up to the ferocity of the sea, sail up the narrow channels of the Firth of Clyde or the Firth of Forth, to deposit their cargoes at Glasgow, Leith or Grangemouth. At Dundee, Aberdeen and many other smaller ports and wharfs, wares from all corners of the world arrive and the products of Scottish agriculture and industry set out on their long journeys.

The ferries, steamers and merchant ships have been joined increasingly in recent years by small boats. Yachting has become very popular, particularly among the inhabitants of towns on the Clyde coast, such as Helensburgh: the Firth and its adjoining sea lochs and their islands, Arran for example, provide interesting crusing. The Caledonian and Crinan Canals also attract their fair share of pleasure craft.

123 *left*, 124 *top*, 125 *centre*, 126 *below*.
The fishing boats in Scotland's many small
ports make colourful pictures – especially
since the introduction of brightly-
coloured plastics for protective clothing
and fish boxes. 123 the crew prepares to
winch the night's catch ashore from
WK 53, the 'Paxonia', at Scrabster.
124 WK 270 returns to port after a night's
fishing in the Pentland Firth. 125 Giant
gulls dive and swoop around the boats
as they anchor offshore to clean and gut
the fish. The gulls wait – not very
patiently – for the fishermen to throw the
rubbish overboard. Greedy gulls,
however, will try every possible way of
snatching whole fish from the decks.
126 As evening draws near, KY 207 is
ready for another night's work.

127, 128, 129, 130 Scapa Flow will mean a great deal to the
many thousands of veterans of the First and Second World
Wars. Scapa was the home of the British Fleet—a large bay
enclosed by the islands of Hoy, Lambholm and South
Ronaldsay, and the Orkney Mainland. It was here that the
Imperial German Fleet was scuttled after the First World
War—under the disbelieving gaze of the British naval
authorities and a group of local schoolgirls. Here too H.M.S.
Royal Oak was sunk by a U-boat in the Second World War.
After the sinking of the Oak, block ships were sunk in some
of the many channels into Scapa, and later huge stone
barriers were built across the gaps to close them forever.
These 'Churchill Barriers' served a dual purpose—for the first
time they sealed the Flow except for two vital channels and,
also for the first time, they provided a safe all-weather link
between the islands via the roadways that were built on top
of them. The Barriers were built by the Italian prisoners of
war at Camp 60 on Lambholm. They were also responsible
for the delightful little chapel only a hundred yards or so
away built in 1944 out of two army huts. The two reminders
of the war at Scapa Flow—the block ships and barriers and
the chapel—provide us with two sharply contrasting
mementos.

131 and **132** *top left, top right:* On the Ayrshire coast stands the ruined castle of Dunure, set above jagged rocks that form part of the Clyde estuary. From the castle rock, on a clear day, the view stretches far out past Arran and into the Firth. Near Dunure is the famous 'electric brae', a road which, when viewed in an uphill direction, looks as if it is running downhill. This curious effect is attributed to the configuration of the countryside and surrounding hills which collectively produce an optical illusion.

133 *right:* The visitor to Skye from the Scottish mainland crosses the Kyle to land at the village of Kyleakin. This view of the fishing boats at Kyleakin pier, with Castle Moil in the background is his first glimpse of the 'Misty Isle'. Castle Moil, a small keep, is reputed to have been the home of a Norse king who levied tolls on all who passed through the Kyle.

134 *far right:* The sand dunes of Lundin Links in the foreground contrast with the industrial skyline of Methil, one of Fife's more industrialised ports.

135: *top left*: Overlooking the North Sea at St. Monance stands the little fourteenth-century church of St. Monans—the latter being the medieval name. The church stands close to the site of the original thirteenth-century shrine and was, in medieval times, a Dominican friary. Today it consists of transepts, a choir and a tower, and it is probable that this was its total extent even in the fourteenth century: there is certainly no trace of any nave. The seas can be wild on this rugged coast, and in storms the lashing waves throw their spray right up to the church walls.

136 *top right*: In sharp contrast, the smooth waters of Luce Bay on the Solway Firth conceal their treachery. The silent tides of Scotland's south-west corner bring with them the dangers of quicksands.

137 *above left*: Loch Fyne is one of Scotland's many west-coast sea lochs although it shares the placid appearance of most of its inland neighbours. Inveraray, nestling close to the loch, has a waterside frontage of Georgian houses and splendid views of the surrounding hills. Small boats lie at anchor in the calm waters around the pier.

138 *above left:* By the side of the River Eye, a fishing boat is being refitted in the border port of Eyemouth. Across the river in this east-coast town is the fish-market where the daily catches of cod, haddock and plaice are offered for sale.

139 *above:* The island of Inchcolm was a well-chosen site for an abbey. When the Augustinians built their monastery here in the twelfth century they relied on the fact that the island's inaccessibility across Mortimer's Deep would safeguard them from attack. Their wise choice has been of paramount importance in preserving the abbey. A small boat carries visitors out to the island. The abbey, except for the church, has survived virtually intact. Most of the monastic buildings are in an impressive state of preservation – even the roofs on the chapter-house, cloisters and other buildings are still in perfect condition. This site was too remote for stone-thieves throughout the centuries since the Reformation. Only the building of a dwelling-house near-by caused part of the abbey to be demolished. In the Second World War, Inchcolm was an important defence post, and remaining signs of the former military presence can be seen on the hill from which this photograph was taken.

140 The fishermen mending their nets at the harbour in Dunbar are carrying on a centuries-old tradition. Although their nets are now made of nylon, the methods used for repairing them have remained virtually unchanged.

141 Scotland's south-east coast is rockier and more forbidding than that further north. It is these high rocks that provide shelter for the fishing fleet in Dunbar harbour. The quiet haven is overlooked by the ruins of the fourteenth-century castle. It was to Dunbar Castle that Mary Queen of Scots and the Earl of Bothwell fled in 1567. A few days after arriving at Dunbar, Mary surrendered to her nobles. Her flight had taken her from Borthwick to Dunbar and then to Carberry Hill where she was taken prisoner after Bothwell fled. On 15th June 1567 she embarked on the course which was to take her first to Loch Leven Castle, then to her escape to England and, finally, up the steps to the scaffold after eighteen years of imprisonment.

142 *below:* St. Abbs Head is the last real look at Scotland's coastline offered to the traveller as he drives south to England. Amidst the towering rocks and cliffs, the little village of St. Abbs appears precariously balanced. This photograph of the cliffs was taken from the hills above the village. At St. Abbs the rocks themselves form the outer protective shell that is the harbour.

143 Dunblane, now rapidly expanding, was until five or six years ago one of Scotland's smallest cities. The old town, built round the magnificent cathedral, contains some delightful buildings. The Dean's House, now the cathedral museum, was the home of the Episcopal dean in the seventeenth century.

7 The Villages & Towns

In Scotland the village is a tradition rather than a picturesque institution. There is no parallel in Scotland to the quaint villages of whitewashed thatched cottages which are to be found in the South of England.

Traditional Scottish architecture is functional and only Fife can be called picturesque—the traditional white harled cottages which abound in the county are almost unique in Scotland and confined mainly to Fife, the Forth estuary and selected areas of Tayside. Any other exceptions are so few that they can be easily counted.

In many cases it is the tradition behind the architecture rather than the buildings themselves which demands our attention. Few villages survive as complete units designed with an overall character—Culross, Dunkeld, Cramond and Inveraray are all that immediately spring to mind. For the remainder it is an individual building or legend that commends them to the visitor. Many of the villages sprang up outside the walls of abbeys; for example Arbroath, Culross, Dunkeld and Elgin; some developed around castles, for example Stirling, Doune, Linlithgow and Blackness. Others—Crail, Pittenweem, Anstruther, Wick, Scrabster, Eyemouth, St. Abbs and many more—developed out of man's need to fish for his food in the sea.

The Roman occupation of Scotland also laid the foundations of many present-day communities. The deserted forts left by the Romans afforded shelter to the local inhabitants who, after a time, left their fortified dwellings to build on the adjacent lands. Braco, a little village in Tayside, owes its development to the immense Roman station at Ardoch nearby.

Stromness, the port at which the Orkney steamer arrives, is a quaint little place although the buildings themselves do not warrant any particular notice. The buildings, huddled together along the seashore, sometimes jutting out on artificial foundations over the water, are linked together in a tight group and are served by narrow paved streets which twist through the houses in a manner which suggests the town came into existence by accident rather than by design. On one side is the sea, on the other steep hills—and in between, Stromness. Contrasting with this is the geometric accuracy of Georgian Inveraray set along the side of Loch Fyne, a curious town where quite ordinary buildings combine to form a picturesque unit.

The villages and towns of Scotland are not merely collections of buildings: they are tightly knit communities of warm, friendly people, each of whom usually knows everybody else. Once a year they congregate at the annual Highland Gathering for a huge contest of strength and skill in which a lot of reputations are put to the test, both on the field and in the beer tent! The ritual of the Highland Games causes both interest and amazement to visitors. The endless dancing contests on a small wooden stage carry on throughout the afternoon while, nearby, strong men throw hammers, toss cabers and heave enormous iron balls through the air. Events include hundred-yard dashes in which the ages of the competitors can be as far apart as twelve and sixty, and cycle races share the track. The expected extravaganza of tartan and of pipe bands is much in evidence, of course. At the day's end, the crowds drift away as the pipe band marches, playing, into the dusk, and normality returns.

144, 145, 146, 147 Fife has numerous charming little
villages, none more attractive than Culross, a fine example
of the domestic architecture of Scotland in the sixteenth and
seventeenth centuries. The village is almost entirely in the
care of, and preserved by, the National Trust for Scotland.
In addition to the village with its 'Palace' there are the ruins
of the thirteenth-century Cistercian abbey. The development
of Culross as a burgh and a port was entirely the result of the
growing industries of salt-panning and coal-mining. Both
industries, started by the Cistercians, were after the
Reformation developed as private enterprises. The local hills
yielded their coal without difficulty and in the late sixteenth

and early seventeenth centuries mining in the shallow pits was encouraged by Sir George Bruce. Culross Palace – a corruption of the word 'Place' – was Sir George's home, a fine stone building with the traditional red roof and crow-stepped gables. The Palace was built in 1611 and contains some fine painted wood panelling. The Mercat Cross, standing in a little cobbled square, is surrounded by the white-harled cottages that are so much a feature of Fife. The present Cross, built in 1902, stands on the site of the original which was erected in 1588, the year the burgh was granted its royal charter by James VI. In our photograph, the Cross is seen before a building known as The Ark, in front of

which runs Mid Causeway. The Study on the opposite side of the square was built around 1600 and now houses offices of the National Trust for Scotland.

148 The narrow winding streets of Stromness come as a sharp surprise to the visitor from the mainland. The streets, paved and without pavements, are shared by motorists and pedestrians alike. Surprisingly there has not been an accident there for years.

149 *top right: Kyleakin, Skye*
The picturesque village which forms the most usual 'gateway to Skye' is a scattered group of cottages and houses along the shore of the Kyle and the small burn which flows into it.

150 Looking through the gates of Dunkeld Cathedral, one can see the little houses of the old city. The cathedral, of which only the choir is now used, can be traced back to the ninth century although the fabric of the present building is mainly of thirteenth- and fourteenth-century origin. The nave of the church is now a ruin. Parklands surround the cathedral and stretch down to the side of the fast-flowing River Tay. Walking down into the town from the church gates, the visitor passes many of the restored cottages and houses which are a feature of the city. On one such house an eighteenth-century 'ell' is marked out: this was the Scottish measure equivalent to a yard and exceeded three feet by a little over an inch.

151 The Cramond Inn is one of a group of beautifully maintained buildings in this little village only five miles from Edinburgh Castle. The River Almond meets the Forth in front of seventeenth-century harled houses. The remains of Roman camps can be seen adjacent to the village churchyard.

152 Traquair House is perhaps one of the oldest inhabited buildings in Scotland. It shares, along with so many other houses and castles, strong links with Mary Queen of Scots. Mary and Darnley – her second husband – stayed here in 1566. From Traquair they moved to Craigmillar Castle where the plot to murder Darnley was evolved. The appearance of this fine turreted house has remained virtually unchanged since the seventeenth century; it is a charming link with the past. The eighteenth-century brewhouse is still operative and ale is made there for sale to visitors.

153 *left:* Throughout Scotland, 'little houses' are restored by the N.T.S. and either rented or sold to persons who undertake to maintain them in their fine condition and to retain the carefully restored traditional appearance. In this way much of Scotland's architectural heritage is being saved from destruction.

156 The royal burgh of Falkland with its beautiful palace offers yet more links with the tragic Queen Mary. James II founded the palace – originally a hunting lodge – in 1450, but it was not extended to its present size until the reign of James V. It was that monarch who built the royal tennis courts in the palace grounds. Royal tennis is unlike lawn tennis but does resemble the modern 'squash'. The royal burgh contains some interesting cottages and houses.

154 and **155** The annual Highland Games at Crieff attract an enthusiastic crowd of over ten thousand people. Our pictures show the Highland dancing competitions and the hammer-throwing contests.

157, 158, 159 The village of Crail is one of those picturesque gems which are the trademark of the East Neuk. Crail has a predominance of charming seventeenth-century buildings closely grouped on the steep hill that drops down to the harbour. Down the little streets revelling in the names of 'Rumford', 'Shoregate' and 'Marketgate' are many buildings of architectural importance; the sixteenth-century Tolbooth and the elegant sixteenth-century Friar's Court are but two. Once again we find crow-stepped gables and red-tiled roofs in abundance. The harbour, with its narrow entrance, is unique in that the great stone slabs which form its walls are laid vertically instead of following the usual horizontal construction. The parish church, once collegiate, dates from the thirteenth century, although many additions, alterations and demolitions throughout the centuries since then have tended to mask much of the original external fabric. Outside the door there is a deeply incised stone set into the wall. The stone bears the scars caused by generations of burghers sharpening their arrow-heads each Sunday after Mass in preparation for their compulsory archery practice. The town has many links with Scotland's history, not least of which is that the harbour was built by one Robert Stevenson – grandfather of Robert Louis Stevenson, the novelist.

160 Dunfermline boasts a fine Norman abbey nave, the ruins of the fourteenth-century palace of the Scots kings and strong ties with King Malcolm and his saintly Queen Margaret. In the choir of the abbey lies Robert the Bruce, while in the palace were born kings, princesses and other royals including David II, James I and Charles I. The palace developed out of the abbey's monastic buildings and was extended in the fourteenth century. After the English King Edward I ordered its destruction in the early fourteenth century, it was almost completely rebuilt by 1315. The last king to live within the walls was Charles II. Unfortunately, the palace today is a mere shell.

PROSPECT OF
SCOTLAND
MAPS

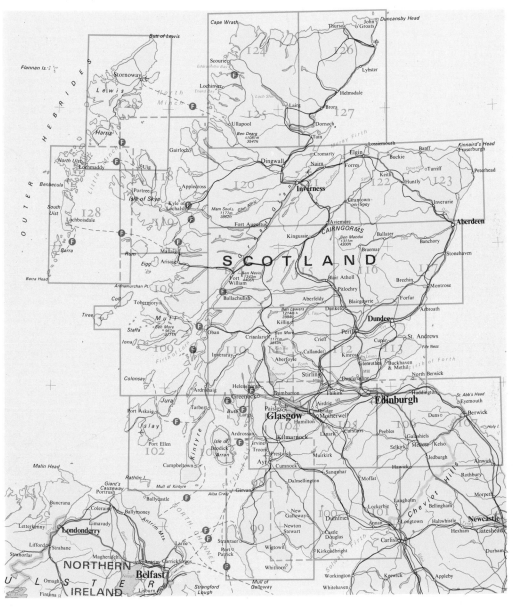

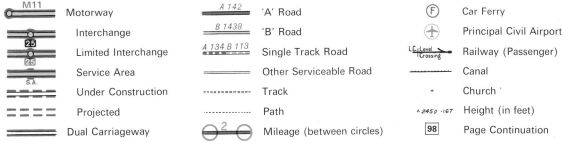

M11 ⊙━━━ Motorway	A 142 ━━━━ 'A' Road	Ⓕ Car Ferry	
⊞ Interchange	B 1438 ━━━ 'B' Road	✈ Principal Civil Airport	
25 Limited Interchange	A 134 B 113 ━━━ Single Track Road	LC Level Crossing ━━━ Railway (Passenger)	
S.A. Service Area	━━━━ Other Serviceable Road	┈┈┈ Canal	
▦▦▦ Under Construction	┄┄┄┄ Track	+ Church	
▬ ▬ ▬ Projected	⋯⋯⋯ Path	△ 2450 · 167 Height (in feet)	
━━━ Dual Carriageway	⊖━2━⊖ Mileage (between circles)	98 Page Continuation	

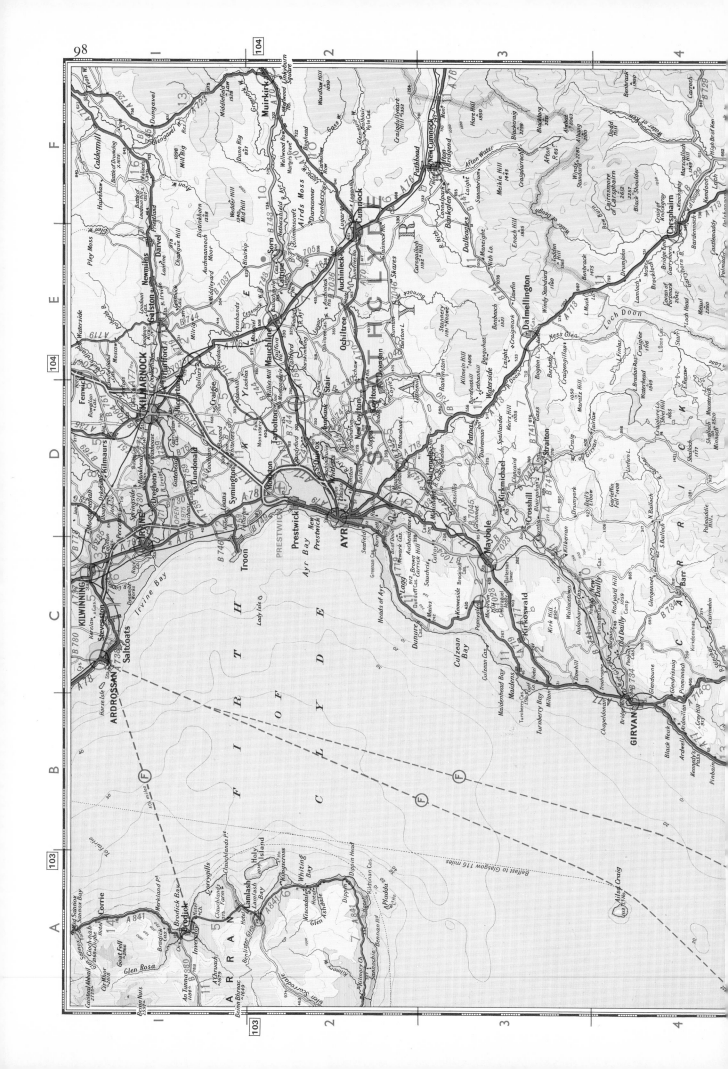

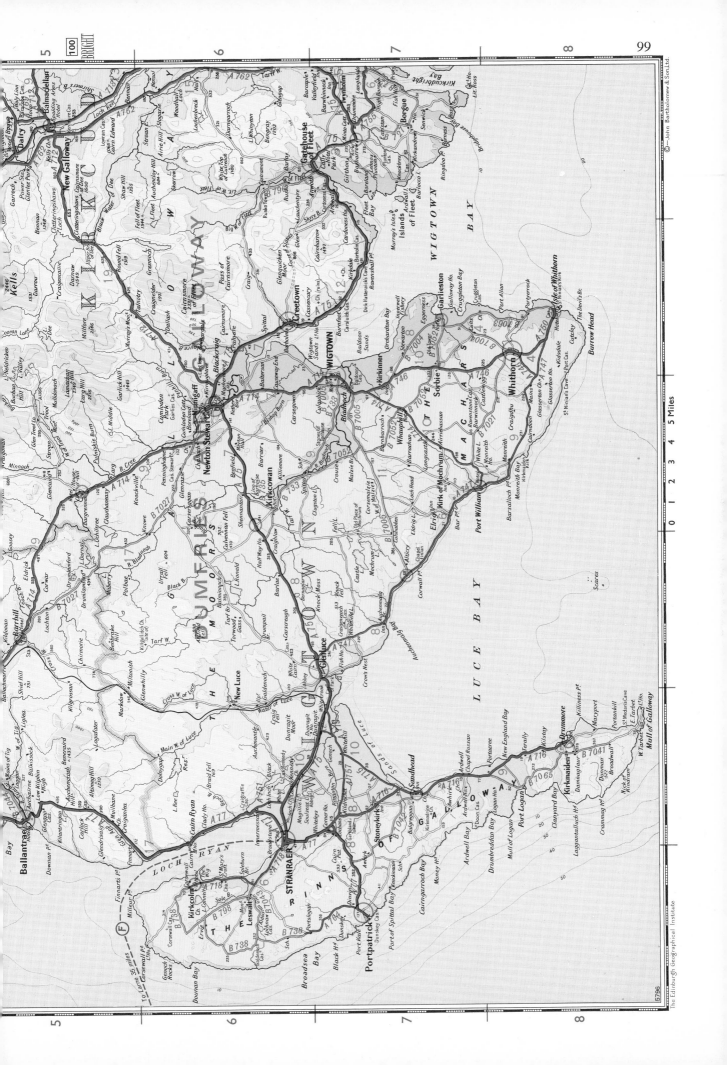

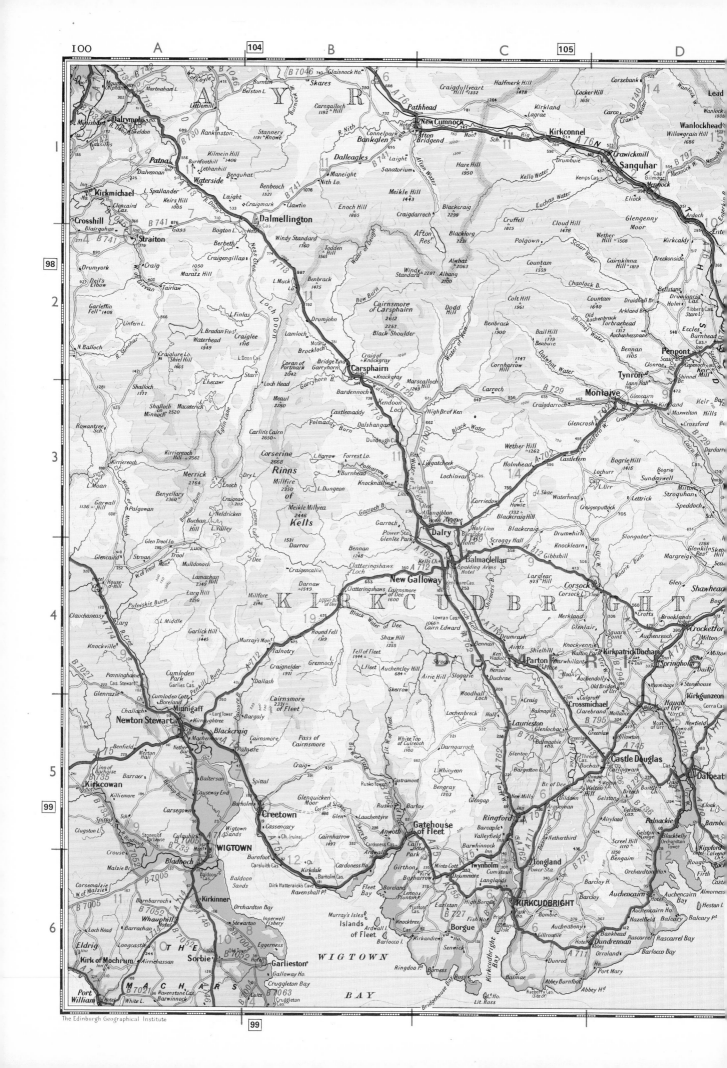

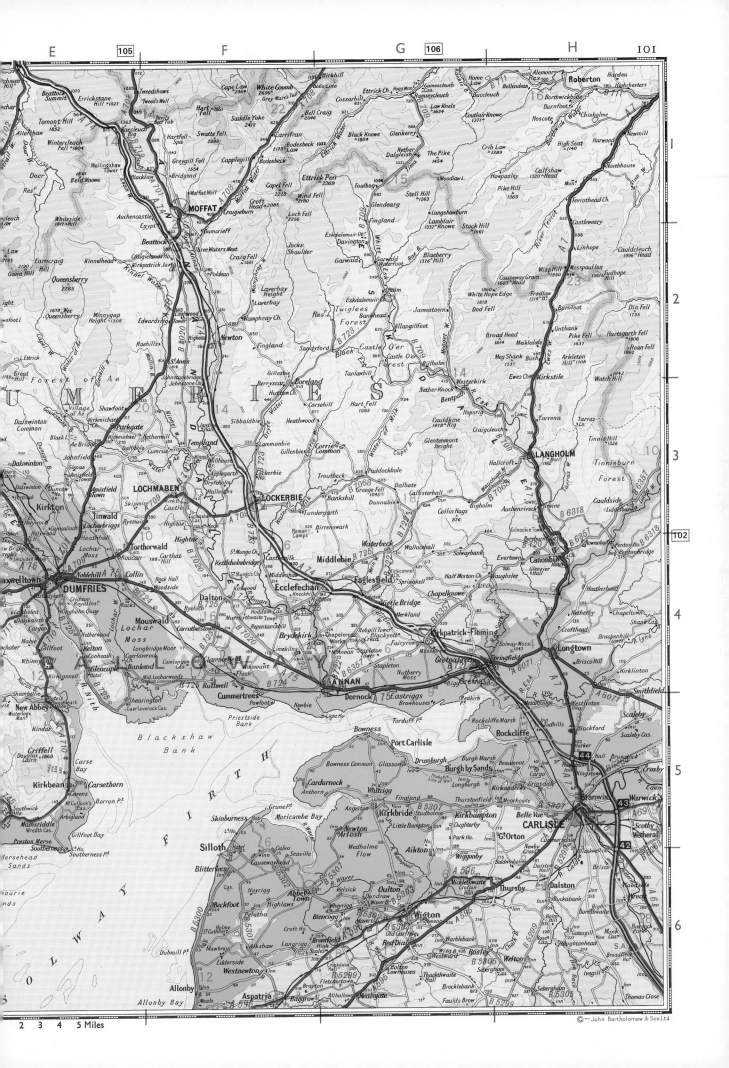

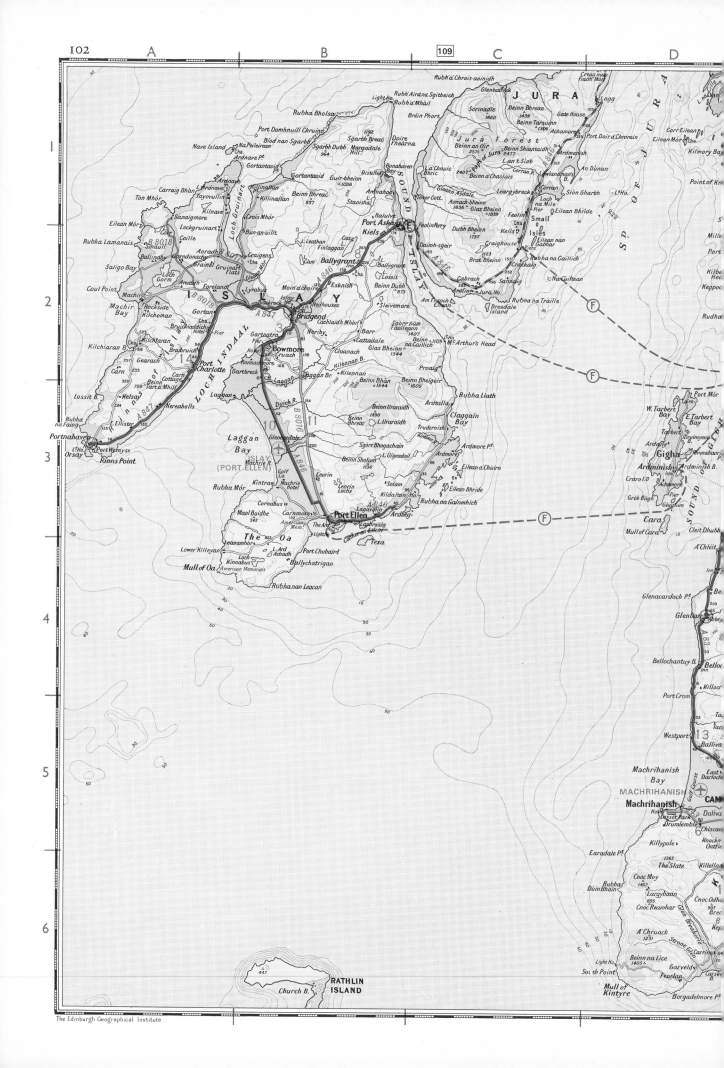

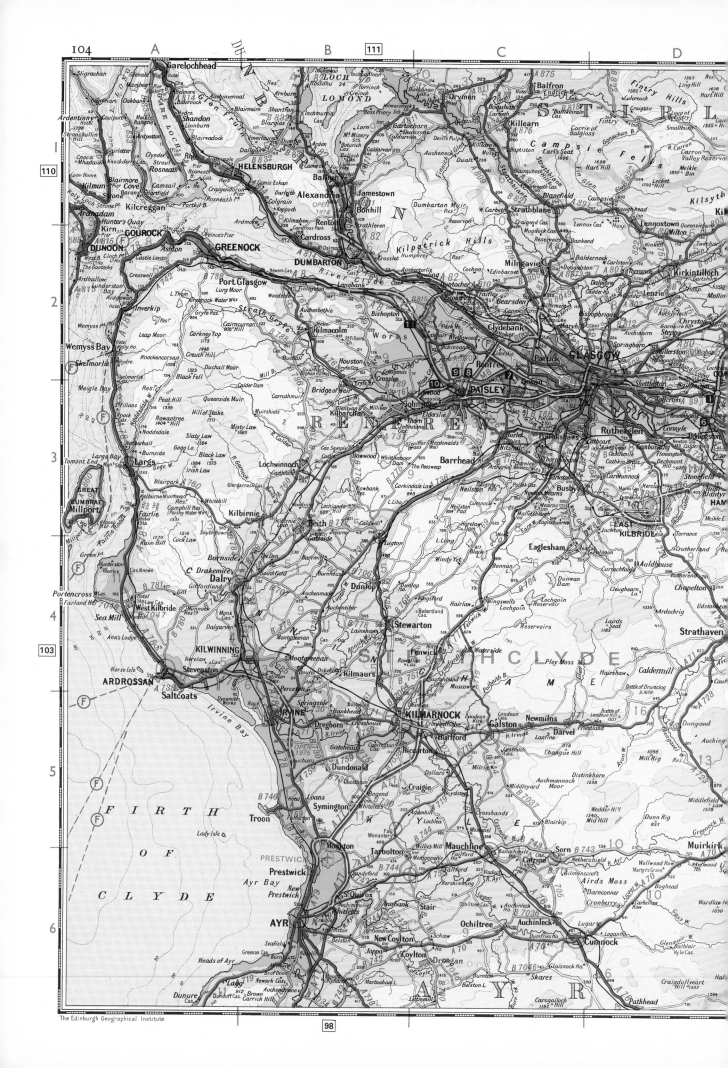

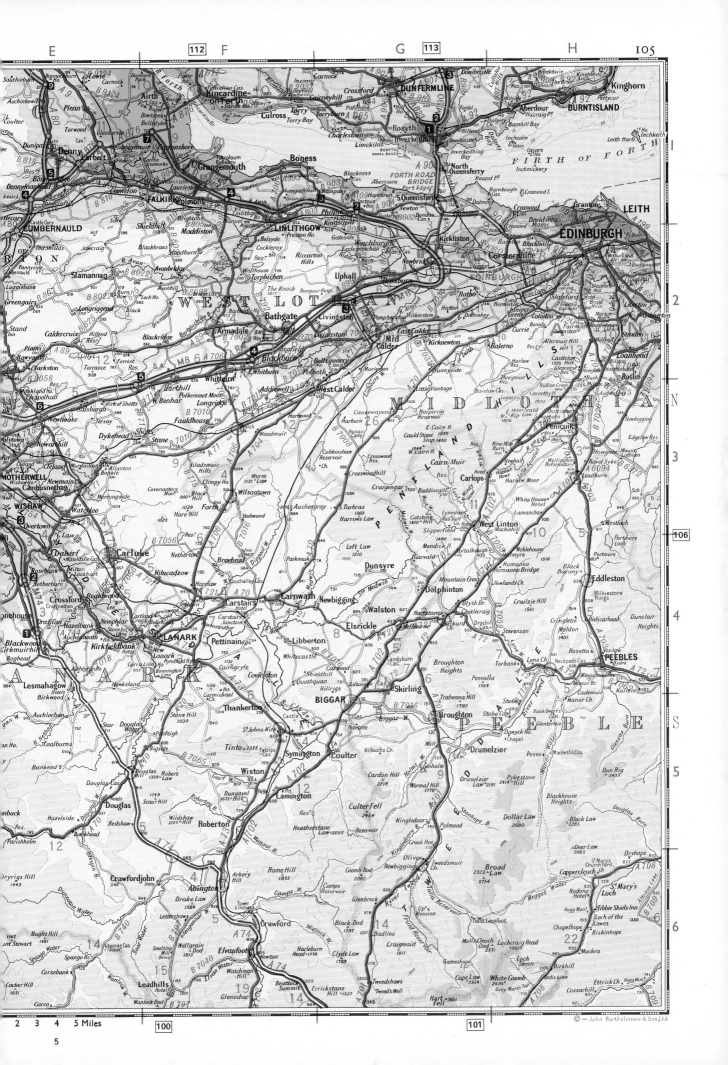

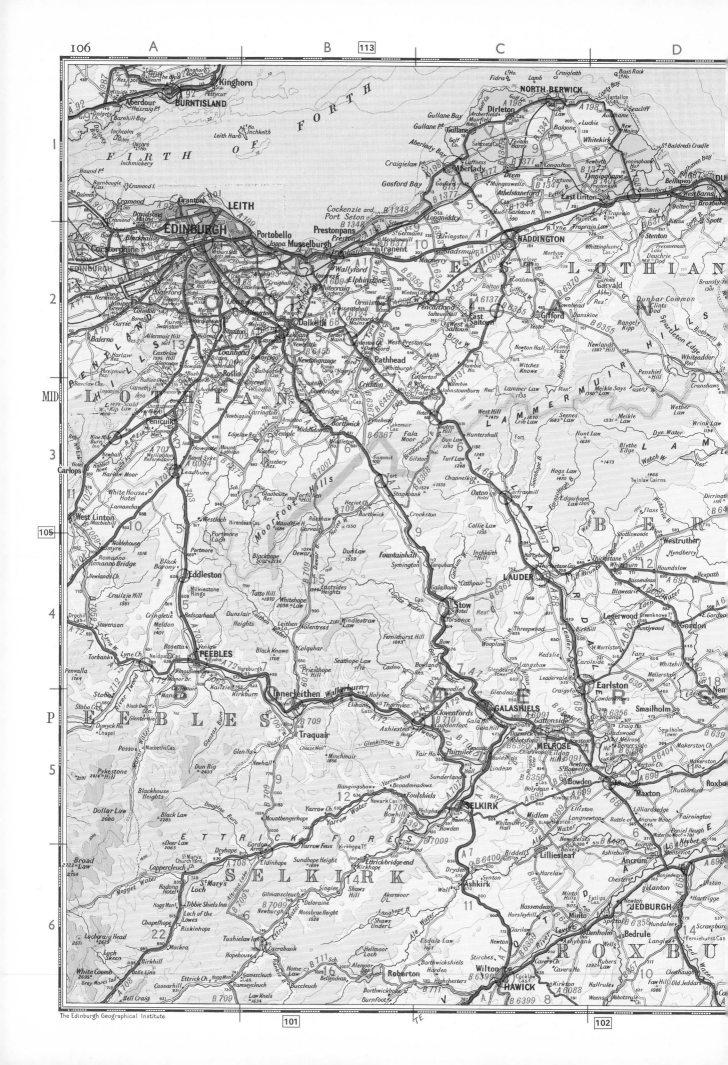

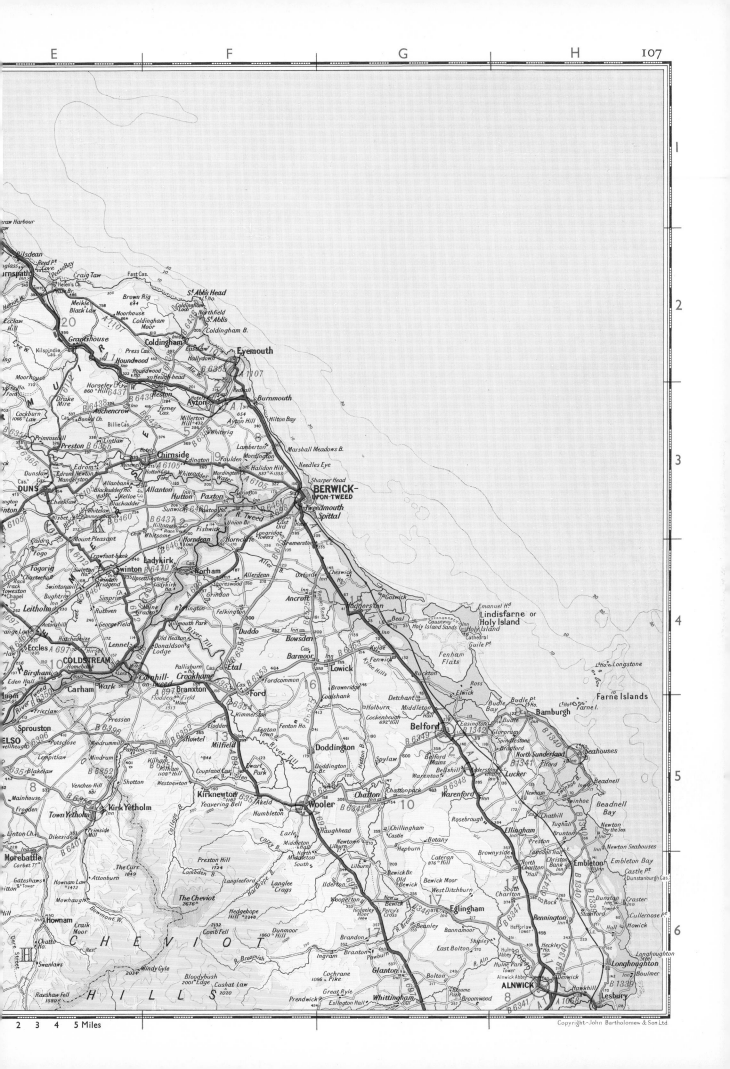

E　　　　　　F　　　　　　G　　　　　　H

1

2

3

4

5

6

Bilsdean
Reed Pt
Cove
Peasebay
urnspath
Craig Taw
Helen's Ch.
Fast Cas.
St. Abb's Head
Meikle
Black Law
Brown Rig
644
A 1107
Grantshouse
Kilspindie Cas.
Coldingham
Moor
Moorhouse
Northfield
St. Abb's
Coldingham B.
Coldingham
Houndwood
Inn
Eyemouth
Horseley Hill
Reston
Ayton
Burnmouth
Auchencrow
Ayton Hill
Hilton Bay
Primrosehill
Preston
Whiterig
Chirnside
Lamberton
Marshall Meadows B.
DUNS
Edrom
Mordington
Halidon Hill
Needles Eye
Whiteadder
Water
Hutton
Paxton
BERWICK-
UPON-TWEED
Allanton
Mount Pleasant
R. Tweed
Tweedmouth
Spittal
East
Ord
Sharper Head
Crowfoot-bank
Ladykirk
Horndean
Horncliffe
Cheswick
Coldstream
Swinton
Norham
Allerdean
Goswick
Felkington
Ancroft
Haggerstan
Beal
Holy Island Sands
Lindisfarne or
Holy Island
Eccles
Lennel
Duddo
Bowsden
Kyloe
Fenwick
Fenham
Flats
Birgham
Cornhill-
on-Tweed
Etal
Barmoor
Lowick
Buckton
Ross
Elwick
Farne Islands
Carham
Wark
Crookham
Ford
Branxton
Flodden Field
Brownridge
Detchant
Middleton
Budle
Bay
Bamburgh
Sprouston
Milfield
Fenton
Holburn
Cockenheugh
Belford
Easington
North Sunderland
Seahouses
Kirknewton
Akeld
Wooler
Chatton
Warenford
Lucker
Newham
Beadnell
Kirk Yetholm
Yeavering Bell
Humbleton
Earle
Chillingham
Castle
Rosebrough
Ellingham
Beadnell
Bay
Town Yetholm
Middleton
Hepburn
Brownyside
Preston
Newton
by the Sea
Morebattle
Preston Hill
Old Bewick
Bewick Moor
West Ditchburn
South Charlton
Embleton
Embleton Bay
Castle Pt
The Cheviot
2676
Hedgehope
Hill
Dunmoor
Hill
New
Bewick
Percy's
Cross
Eglingham
Rennington
Craster
Cullernose Pt
Hownam
Comb Fell
Brandon
Branton
Bannamoor
Shipley
Heckley
Howick
CHEVIOT
Windy Gyle
Bloodybush
Edge
Cushat Law
Cochrane
Pike
Great Ryle
Glanton
Bolton
R. Aln
Hulne Park
Tower
Berwick
Longhoughton
Boulmer
HILLS
Raeshaw Fell
Prendwick
Eslington Hall
Whittingham
ALNWICK
Hawkhill
Lesbury

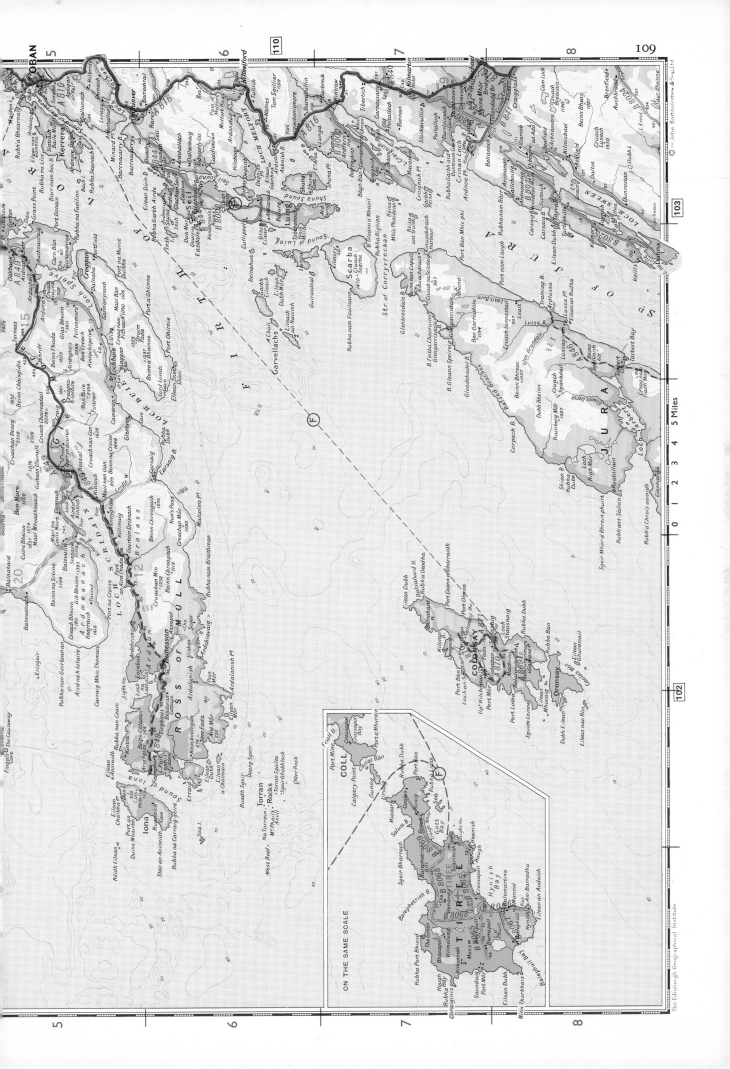

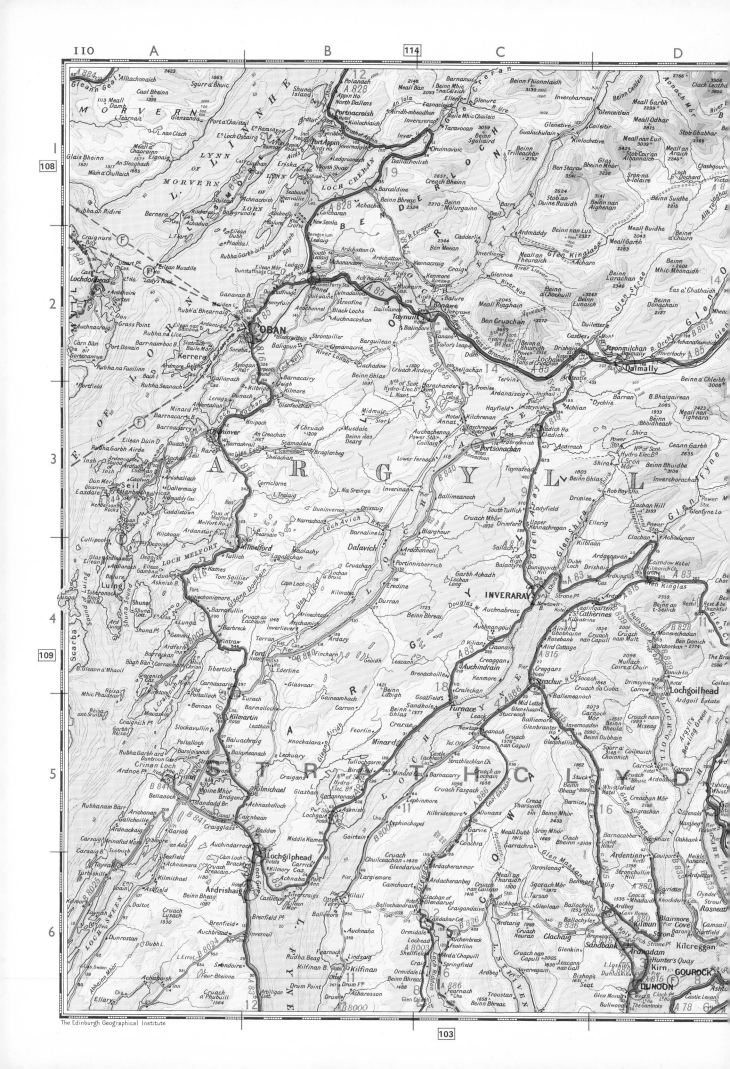

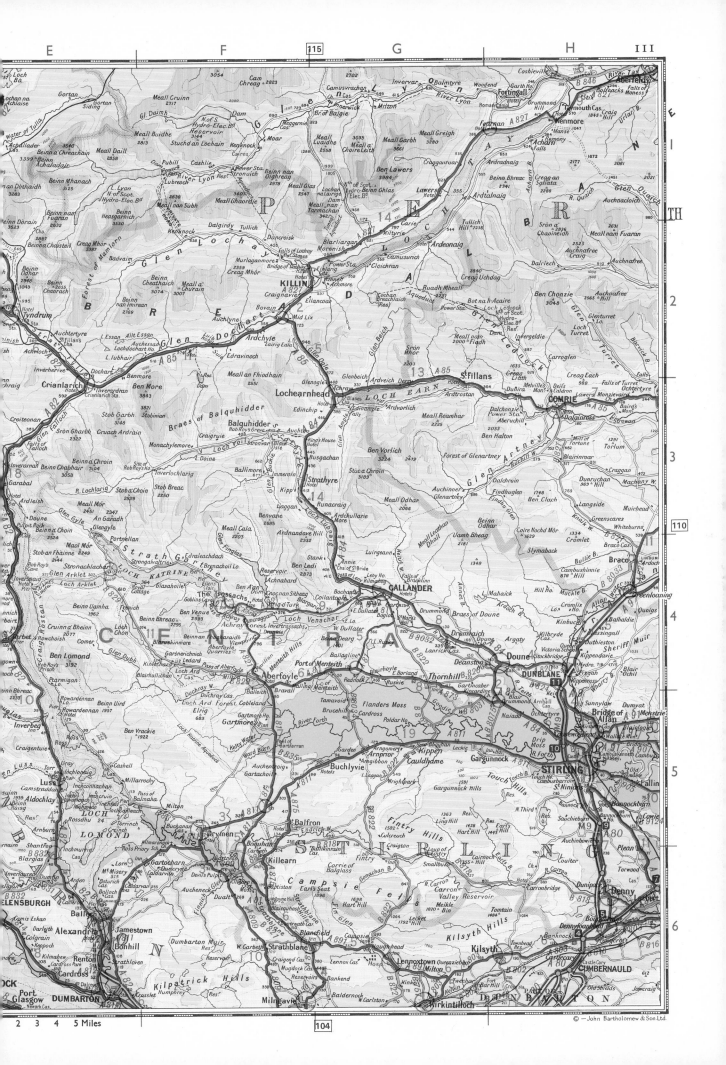

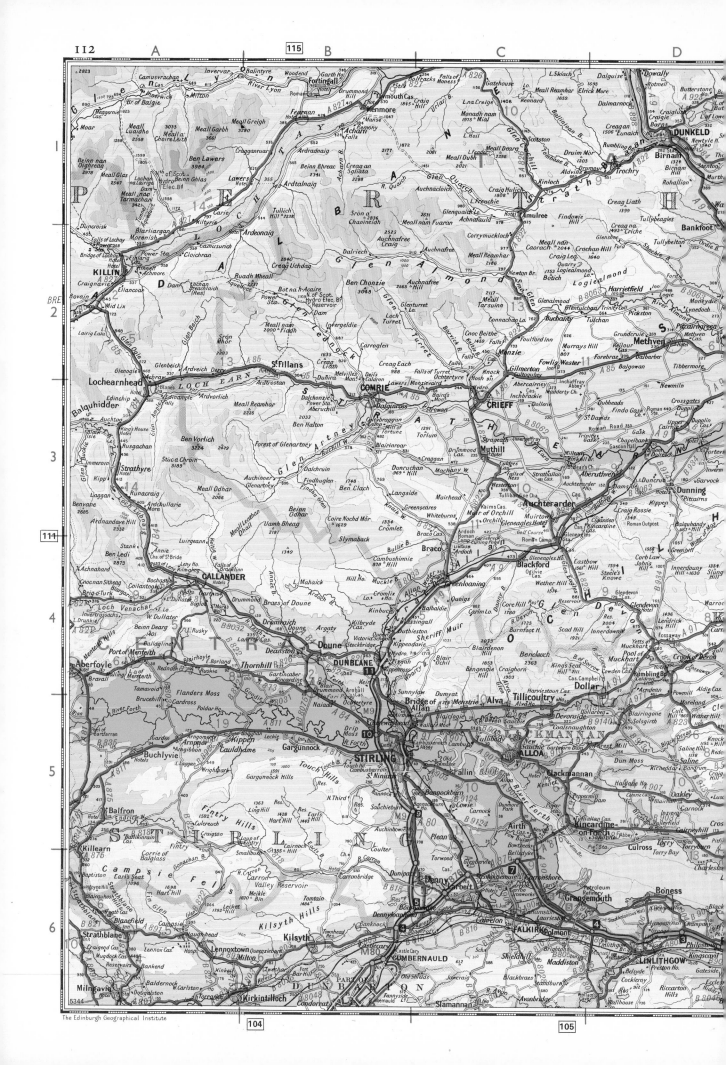

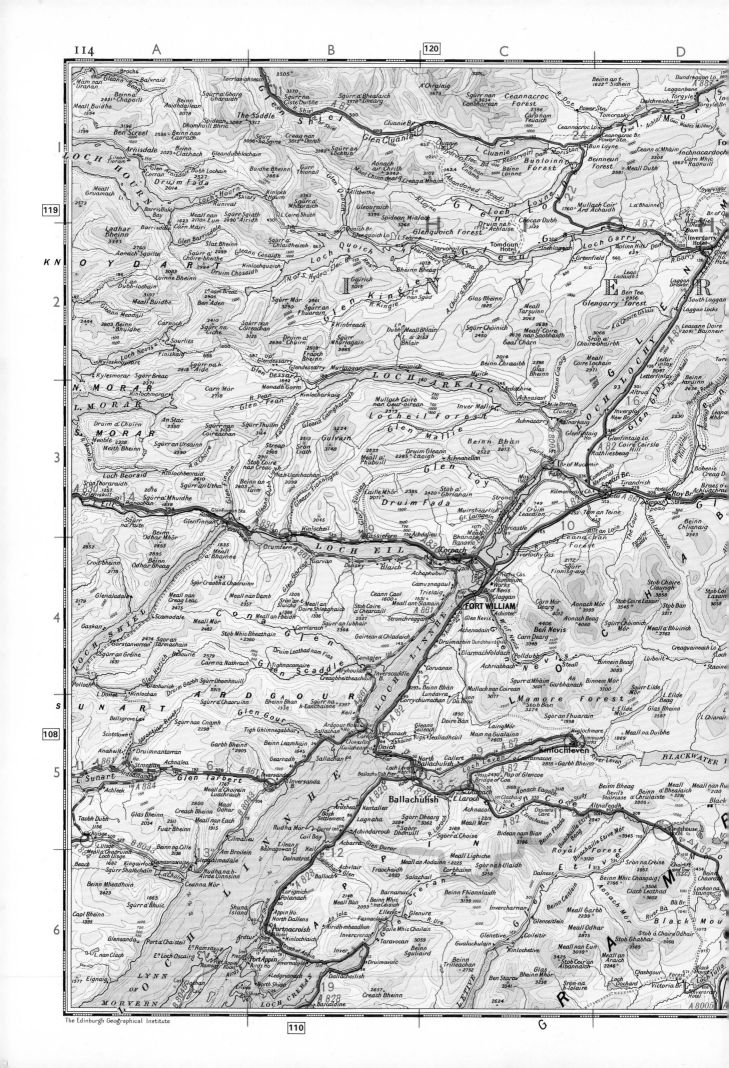